IMMERSIVE THEATRE

Engaging the Audience

Josh Machamer, Editor

IMMERSIVE THEATRE

Engaging the Audience

Josh Machamer, Editor

COMMON GROUND RESEARCH NETWORKS 2017

First published by Common Ground Research Networks in 2017
as part of the *Arts in Society Book Imprint*

University of Illinois Research Park
2001 South First Street, Suite 202
Champaign, IL 61820 USA
Ph: +1-217-328-0405
http://cgnetworks.org

Library of Congress Cataloging-in-Publication Data

Names: Machamer, Josh editor.
Title: Immersive theatre : engaging the audience / Josh Machamer, editor.
Description: Champaign, IL : Common Ground Research Networks, 2017. |
Identifiers: LCCN 2016030120 (print) | LCCN 2016049542 (ebook) | ISBN
    9781612299204 (pdf) | ISBN 9781612299181 (hbk : alk. paper) | ISBN
    9781612299198 (pbk : alk. paper)
Subjects: LCSH: Performing arts--Audiences. | Participatory theater.
Classification: LCC PN1590.A9 (ebook) | LCC PN1590.A9 I55 2017 (print) | DDC
    792.02/2--dc23
LC record available at https://lccn.loc.gov/2016030120

Cover Photo Credit:
The Other Shore
by Gao Xingjian, translated by Gilbert C. F. Fong
California Polytechnic State University, San Luis Obispo - 2015
Ian Billings, photographer
Director, Josh Machamer
Costume Design, Thomas John Bernard
Scenic and Lighting Design, Pegi Marshall-Amundsen

Table of Contents

Immersive Theater Practice in Theater for Younger Audiences: Interviews with Three Companies

Adrienne Kapstein

One of the most active and adventurous arenas in contemporary immersive performance is in theater for young audiences. Many of the leading companies making work for children do not consider age a limitation but rather an invitation to challenge traditional theater conventions, such as the relationship between performer and spectator; the audience's role in performance, and the inclusion of the audience-participant into the creative process itself.

For over forty years, Denmark has been a global leader in making quality, sophisticated, and highly experimental work for young audiences. Belgium, The Netherlands, and Australia are also renowned for boundary pushing work in form and content for audiences of children and young people, and with the founding of the Imaginate Festival in 1999, Scotland has become an important global contributor in the performing arts for children. More recently, theater-makers in the US, who had not previously considered children and families an exciting or challenging audience, have started to create work that is more inclusive in terms of age. In the past few years, companies like Pig Iron Theatre Company, The Civilians, and Fiasco Theater have all been presented at The New Victory Theater, the country's premiere venue for national and international children's programming, or developed work as part of The New Victory Lab Works Residency Program (established in 2011–2012). Soho Repertory Theater, considered to be the vanguard of new play development in the US, produced their first family show in 2015, a site-specific, immersive piece entitled *Washeteria*.

Theater for Young Audiences is not a genre. It is a blanket term that encompasses work in every performance style made for a vast range of ages, including recent developments in theater for babies in utero;[1] Theater for the Very Young (TVY)[2] (ages 0–3 years); and all the way up to teenagers. A common trend across this broad age range is that much of the work utilizes immersivity [sic] in some way. As outlined in a recent article by Meg Lowey in TYA Today (*Splash! Diving Into the Waters of Immersive Theatre for Young Audiences*, Spring 2015), audiences of children come to the theater without prior expectations as to what a theater-going experience should entail; what theater should look like or what is expected of them. They are far more

---

[1] Lullaby by Polka Theatre, UK, 2013 and Blooming Voices by The Welsh National Opera, 2012 were shows created for foetuses

[2] In the United Kingdom this sector audience is known as Theater for Early Years (TEY)

ready to take the leap of faith, that is the suspension of disbelief, than adult audiences; their instinctive readiness to *"immerse themselves in adventure"*[3] lends itself to a participatory exchange between the action on stage and/or the site in which the performance occurs. Where an adult audience may need a gradual entry into an immersive experience before they can comfortably partake, an audience of children will willingly enter into the imaginative realm, and indeed at times may need clear definitions drawn to help them separate themselves from the story.

The total sensory engagement that makes immersive performance thrilling and novel to adult audiences is intuitive to an audience of the very young. As pre-verbal beings, babies, and young children are expert at learning about their surroundings through all five senses. Before children are able, or conditioned, to understand a narrative structure, they are at ease with abstract and non-linear experiences which are often a hallmark of immersive work. These qualities, inherent to various stages of childhood development, make the child audience-participant a natural candidate for immersive experiences.

For this chapter, I have interviewed artists from three highly acclaimed companies making work for young people that all use immersivity [sic] in their productions in unique and ground-breaking ways. I have attempted to examine what motivates and inspires these theater-makers to use this form for this audience. The companies are Oily Cart (UK), who create immersive and multisensory performances for children and young people, as well as children with profound and multiple learning disabilities, and those on the autism spectrum; Carte Blanche (Denmark) a company at the forefront of contemporary performance practice in creating immersive, sensorial, and participatory experiences that exist in a realm between theater and installation; and Polyglot Theatre (Australia), a company that creates immersive productions and interactive "Play Space"[4] experiential work.

These companies vary widely—culturally, aesthetically, in their processes, in the specific age ranges, and in the physical and cognitive abilities of their target audiences—but they share a deep consideration of their audience's perspective and are all dedicated to creating work that places the child audience at the very center of the experience. The immersive form is more than an opportunity for aesthetic experimentation for these artists. It is driven by a deep-seated understanding, respect, and curiosity as to how best to engage and move their audiences; an endeavor to construct an imaginative framework that speaks to the child at their own level—thematically, structurally, sensorially, physically, spatially.

By making art that places the child at the heart of the work, these companies are engaged not only in a creative act but a civic one of democratization and advocacy. In making work with the highest artistic standards, these companies are honoring children as creative beings in their own right able to engage with art in complex and meaningful ways. The immersive and participatory form is a direct and deliberate act of communication and connection with the child audience. By speaking to these

---

[3] Jonathan Shmidt-Chapman, Artistic Director, of Trusty Sidekick Theater Company, a New York-based company dedicated to making work for young people. Formed only five years ago, Trusty Sidekick has become internationally recognized as a company making innovative, immersive site-specific and site-responsive work.

[4] "Play-space works" is how Sue Giles, Artistic Director of Polyglot refers to this strand of her company's work. Interview with Adrienne Kapstein, 12/28/2015

audience members of young people in the best way that can be "heard"; by not privileging the traditional theater-going conventions nor hierarchizing spoken text or linear narrative as the only means of storytelling, but instead honoring all forms of "language" to facilitate communication and create shared experiences, immersivity [sic] becomes necessary and essential.

OILY CART, LONDON, UK

For almost thirty-five years, Oily Cart have been at forefront of defining and redefining what theater can look like and who it can be made for. The company has been utilizing immersive, interactive, and multi-sensory storytelling techniques from the start. They began creating shows for the very young (under five year olds), and in the late 1980s expanded to include work for young people on the low functioning side of the autism spectrum and for those defined as having profound and multiple physical and learning difficulties (PMLDs). These include a range of sensory and cognitive impairments; audience members often have medical support needs and mobility issues. Oily Cart uses the stimulation of any and every sense as a possible entry point for their audience. They create shows using aromas, vibrations, taste, touch, and movement; shows where participants, musicians, and performers are immersed in water; on trampolines; suspended by bungees, and installed inside of enormous drums. They have made work that lasts one or two weeks allowing for relationships to build—for the performers to learn about the audience; the audience to learn about the performers and the performance experience itself. Oily Cart recognizes that its audience is not just composed of young people, but includes the parents, teachers, and caregivers that accompany children to the theater, and when performing for audiences with PMLDs, the audience also includes the intimate and complex network of caregivers, medical support aids, and family members. Tim Webb, Artistic Director of Oily Cart says of their audience that it is, "*A far greater range than you would ever find in the stalls of the national theaters.*"[5]

Excerpts from Interview with Tim Webb, Artistic Director and co-founder, Oily Cart:

AK: Can you describe Oily Cart's approach to theater? And how did you discover the immersive form? Was it the form before the audience or the audience before the form?

TW: To get to the nitty-gritty, the work is really very multisensory. And it doesn't rely on the theater standbys of vision and hearing. We are very interested in introducing smell into our work and introducing tactile things, the kinesthetic sense, the sense that the body has of its own movement, and the relation of the body parts to one another. We've got a show about the different smells that accompany particular episodes. There's an episode in a garden. There's an episode in a laundry. And at each point, we are introducing the young people and their families—because they're of

---

[5] Tim Webb in interview with Adrienne Kapstein 12/22/15

very great importance in the whole equation—to things that are not normally part of the language of theater.

This is the part of our theater that originated with the young people, in particular, who are on the autism spectrum. We're looking for ways in which we can move them into our shows, our performances, so that the shows are co-created by *them*. So, we are asking young people—if they use verbal language, "what do we do next?" or in terms of the crisis, "what's going on?" Or we're asking them to make choices between this smell or that smell or this texture or that texture. Because we don't see them as passive consumers of the work. Especially with the people on the autism spectrum, or those with profound and multiple learning disabilities, they have very different ways of being in the world, probably than the ways that you and I have. We think it's very important to reflect that. And the feedback we get both directly from the kids, which you can perceive, but also the people who work or live with the kids (the parents and their teachers), is that it's this sort of acceptance that there are equally valid ways of living on planet earth that has a profound effect on them. Our theater acknowledges and honors that. In fact, revels in it. And it works. Parents with kids on the autism spectrum often say that they feel that their offspring are living in a sort of parallel world, or in a bubble, or an expression like that. But if you're in an Oily Cart production, the world is a world that accepts both the view of the parent and also the view of the child because we mold to them.

We do a technique, which is called Intensive Interaction, which is taught in the UK, particularly by a fabulous woman called Phoebe Caldwell as a means of communicating with people who have no conventional language apparently. But in fact, everyone it seems does have a language, which might be a language of gesture, it might be a language of sounds or vocalizations and you can perceive the patterns in the sounds and in the gesture and realize that this is someone who, like probably all of us, needs to be able to communicate to feel that you're not all alone in the great, wide universe. [This is an] important aspect of Oily Cart, which is that we've always seen ourselves as identifying an audience and then trying to find a way in which we can communicate with that audience. People who are often isolated, and the people who love the ones who are also isolated [say], "Oh my God, this is actually happening, my child, my student is not alone. There are people who are at least trying to set up plans of communication." And that's what drives us on really—to try and get better at doing that. And it works often enough to keep us going.

AK: Not all immersive work is interactive—you're not always invited to touch or play even though you might be surrounded by the performance. But it sounds like in Oily Cart's work there's really no distinction between the two and that interactivity is something that is being searched for on any level, by any means, at all times. Does that seem right?

TW: Yes, yes. Thinking back, when we started doing work for under-fives, we realized [they] basically have got no idea about a proscenium arch and have no respecter of it. And if we were doing anything that was interesting for a regular old under-fives audience, they wanted to come and join us in the world we've created. They wanted to ask us questions. They wanted to tell us what to do. They wanted to feel the things we were feeling. And at first, we fought it. We were trying to find ways of keeping the kids from coming on stage. But then we thought, well actually it's great, if this stuff's any good they'll want to come on stage with us. Anyway, when you start working with the people who've got profound disabilities and autism, you sort of have to let them engage viscerally and by using their sense of smell and by using their sense of taste. Because there aren't any other ways. You can't just say, "Look at the visuals," you have to have it all there and you have to say, "You can interact with it."

So, the current show called *Land of Lights* which we are doing in the theater for kids from three to five with disability, no disability, it doesn't matter, there is a strong element of interaction. All the stars have fallen out of the sky and we try to find them again. And the gardener says, he thought some stars fell into these flower pots and the kids have to search in these flowerpots and in one or two of them, sure enough there are stars. And then the cook says that he thinks some of the stars must have fallen into his jelly bowls because he heard splashing sounds and so we get twenty-five of them all searching through jelly. So, it's all highly visceral, highly tactile. And then after they have been searching through jelly, you have to clean them up so we've got warm soapy water, warm towels. I just love watching them because they are so committed to the project, finding the stars. And they will do these things because it is necessary and they concentrate and focus. It's a thing of wonder to me that these little kids are just so engaged with the world. So motivated.

The autistic guys particularly, they present a particularly interesting prompt, sort of a challenge, but it's a prompt, where you don't know what aspect of the world that you're going to present that they will be interested in because they're on a different agenda. It's often not people's faces; it's not their voices that the autistic guys are interested in. That poster on the wall, that's got a very interesting shade of red all over it. That might be the thing that my son would be getting off on. As [as] you can't know what part of the environment the young person on the spectrum is on, you feel obliged to try and make everything in there interesting—the ceiling, the floor, the carpet, the walls, the colors, and the smell of the characters…the sound that the characters make. We actually call it 360 degree theater. So, wherever you look, wherever you're looking, whatever you sniff, whatever you touch, it's going be engaging or potentially so for you.

AK: I'm assuming not all the performances have a linear narrative arc. Dramaturgically, how do you shape these performances?

TW: We do this approach which we call "Close-Up/Long-Shot" using cinematic terms. As an individual performer in there working with the parent-child dyad, that's your close-up. That's for them. It's quiet, it's internal, it's very flexible, it's very responsive, and it's usually conducted by the musician. Then, the musician will decide that it's time to move on and then you go to a long shot, which is often a song where you pull back from the close-up relationship and you present something that's more like a theater show. And that's a way of pacing the whole thing, moving it on, and making a show for people on the autistic spectrum. A shared experience. That's what makes it theater.

A show for people on the autism spectrum or for people with very complex disabilities will be quite abstract in a way, but it's definitely got on arc. You can't start off other than by gradually sloping in. We often have a preparatory area outside the main performance space where you will play and where you will gradually meet performers who will then take you into the main performance space. And there again, it will be gentle, it will be well lit, it will be non-threatening. But as you earn the right to have the confidence of the children, then you can become more intense and make greater demands of them. And at about the three-quarter mark, you might have a complete blackout in which you can introduce beautiful lighting effects or wind machines or things like that. Then you come away from that so people feel the experiences definitely and actually ended. You can't just end it. It's a very big mistake *not* to say to an autistic audience, "Okay, the show's about to end, it's going to end in a minute. Oh, it's time to end. Goodbye." You need to come out and then gradually disengage. That's the structure.

AK: You're sculpting the experience it seems.

TW: Very much. Some people will experience what we do as a series of moments. They're living in the moment. They will enjoy playing with the lentils. They'll enjoy putting their heads down the tuba. They will enjoy the perfume sprays. But they won't relate because they don't remember far enough back and they don't speculate about the future. But you don't know, you never know with anybody actually whether that sort of thing is true because you can't read other people's minds. So, we always assume that in fact the people that we are working with are in sort of locked-in syndrome. They are as intelligent as you or I, only they can't express it. So, the thing you have to do is to make work that you find deeply satisfying and make it as well as you can because you don't want any Eleven-year-old kid who's got profound multiple learning disabilities out there thinking "I wish these clowns would bugger off so I could get back to listening to Radio 3." So, it just has to be really good because you don't know. Does it make the hairs on the back of your neck stand up? Well, then the chances are it will make the hairs on somebody else's neck stand up.

CARTE BLANCHE, VIBORG, DENMARK

"In Denmark, children are not perceived as 'becomings' who must learn to understand art, but as 'beings' that have independent artistic experience ability. with the same requirements of good, professional artistic experiences that adults have."[6] Danish theater artist, Sara Topsøe-Jensen, Artistic Director of Carte Blanche, is steeped in this long-standing cultural commitment to children. Young people are valued as an exciting and capable audience able to experience and navigate multiple and experimental theatrical forms and can be exposed to themes and contents that in other Western cultures might be considered off-limits. In Denmark, "No topics are taboo: From harassment, paedophilia, death and destruction to everyday-life, friendship, absurdities and pure comedies."[7]

---

[6] "Theatre for Young Audience as a Tool for Social Engagement in Denmark: An Evaluation of some selected Danish Theatre Companies," A Theatre Research conducted by Theatre Emissary International by Taiwo Okunola Afolabi, published by Statens Kunstrad Danish Arts Council and Theatre Emissary International, 2013, pg. 14
[7] Theater Centrum website *http://www.teatercentrum.dk/danish_theatre_for_young_audiences.asp*

Carte Blanche makes sensory-based work for adults and children (generally ages eight and up) that embeds the audience in the work. Actively resisting generic definition by experimenting with form, the company often blends the tools of immersive theater and art installation. They create elevated, poetic, often sacred-feeling spaces, and carve out opportunities for the participants to encounter the space, the performers, and the other audience members allowing for genuine moments of connection, intimacy, and exchange.

Past shows include *Kalejdoskop* (*Kaleidoscope*), an immersive voyage where the audience like Alice, in *Alice in Wonderland*, collectively falls down the rabbit hole to experience reality as if "*from an atom-particle level or being inside a fractal*"[8]; *Androkles and the Lion* where the audience lies in hammocks under a changing tented "sky" and watches, listens, and feels the myth unfold; and the genre-blurring, trans disciplinary, multi-media work, *Time woke up in Darkness (and walked across the room)*, which utilizes immersive theater, live animation, live music, audience participation, and time itself (the piece lasts for six hours), to explore and investigate time as an abstract and lived experience.

Excerpts of interview with Sara Topsøe-Jensen, Artistic Director, Carte Blanche:

AK: Could you describe and define the work of Carte Blanche?

STJ: Carte Blanche has changed a lot over the ten years that it has existed and one of our attributes is that we keep going to the place where we are curious. Right now, I would say we are creating poetic spaces and this could be scenography inside a black box or it could be an audio guide in the streets or it could be a human-to-human meeting in the library. We are trying to create poetic spaces where humans can meet each other in reality in a bigger, deeper context.

I never set out to do children's theater. I discovered [it] by accident [and] I have come to really appreciate them and love them as very challenging partners in the poetic and artistic meeting. What I like best is if you have a performance where there is an audience of all ages. We tend to not be able to go lower than eight or six years depending on what we're doing, but it touches me a lot if you can make an existential meeting between two human beings, this is also very strong if one human being is twelve years-old and the other one is sixty-five and they allow each other to look at what is death and the reality of death, for example. That's very moving if you do that across ages because we tend to put each other in these existential boxes and have this idea that you grow into being a deeper existential human being when you grow older. [With an audience of all ages] the depth is there from the beginning, if you have the curiosity and the discipline to create the space where [the work] can engage any human being. And of course, we work with the poetic, you could say a mythological poetic aesthetic language, we don't work with an intellectual language.

Theatercentrum is a self-governing institution under the Danish Ministry of Culture that promotes the distribution and dissemination of Danish theatre for young audiences.
[8] Sara Topsøe-Jensen in interview with Adrienne Kapstein 1/11/2016

AK: How do you build immersive work? When and how do you invite the audience participant into process?

STJ: I worked only with a child audience for many years in our rehearsal periods, then I think two years ago, we wanted to do a performance only for adults, because there are limitations for both. And for the first time for many years, we invited an audience of adults in during our rehearsal periods and it was like a cold bucket of water in the face. I mean the children take what is there and they respond very strongly to your presence. So even if I'm there with a scrubby scenography and I'm not at all finished—everybody who works with art knows that it's a very fragile period. The children are very good at following you into that space because they deal with what is there. I actually see it as a tool that we have to use.

When we do performances, I would say one third of our rehearsal period is with a test audience. This is for me kind of the basis of immersive theater. I can rehearse a scene with myself if I'm performing or dancing [but] I never know how it works until it hits the audience. The way that we work with immersive theater, I literally cannot perform my scene if there is not an audience because I would move around how the audience would move, or I would try to make them go with me to do this or I would explore something with them. It has to be improvised with an audience and no matter if we do a performance targeted for adults or children, we always test it on both adults and children because they have different abilities.

It's very, very joyful and wonderful to invite children into a rehearsal period, because they're not, and I mean this in a good sense, because they're not critical, they're not pointing at all the things that are not finished; we can say to them "Okay, it's not really as dark as we want it and we don't have costumes and we don't really know what we're gonna to, but let's play," and they just [say], "Okay." And then you can actually feel what's working, where that is much more difficult with an adult audience, because they need the whole thing to be finished before they can forget themselves in it. So, actually the child audience is a very big part of developing our work.

It's become fashionable to do immersive theater. If it's immersive it's kind of like a plus already, [but] I think sometimes people are not critical enough in terms of how difficult it actually is to really make it work. Where I think that immersive theater really works is if I spontaneously just do something and that is what the room wants me to do. Or I go where my curiosity takes me. I hate when I feel like I'm a this side player. What is this word?

AK: An extra.

STJ: An extra. I hate it when I feel like I'm an extra in somebody else's artistic work. Because on one hand, you have an audience who comes into [a] world you created, so you know the rules. And what we do as an audience, we really want it to succeed. So, you can do immersive theater and it will work really well, everybody will do the right thing, but they will do it to help you be a success. And we [Carte Blanche] are very curious and careful to *really* feel and ask the audience how their experience was, because we're not interested in them helping us doing a performance. We're interested in providing a room where we turn on a curiosity and a questioning and then they follow. But they have to have a feeling that it's their own curiosity, and we provide the space where this curiosity is being pushed and met and challenged. What we are trying to do is to make what's happening on the inside of the audience active. So, I really like the word 'immerse'; it's not something you experience looking outside, you are totally in it.

AK: Could you talk more about this idea of human-to-human; audience-to-audience discovery and connection in your work?

STJ: Some eight years ago was the first time that I was curious about, "How can we make the audience meet each other?" So, it's not about the audience meeting me or another performer, but, "How can we make strangers see each other and be moved and touched and fall in awe, for another human being?" And for me, this right now is what I'm and Carte Blanche is all about. To re-discover the beauty of reality in each other and this touches me so much. When we succeed in creating this room, where we're kind of like the host, but we stand in the background and you see two strangers have a meeting that's very strong and deep and they don't know each other. To be very invisible, you have to move all the attention away from you and the room, and put the attention in what's happening in the audience and between the audience.

Life Live! was a co-production with another company that works with immersive theater called Cantabile 2 here in Denmark [and this show] was very much about the human-to-human meeting. It was interesting because Nullo Facchini, who is the Artistic Director of Cantabile 2, has developed his own very interesting immersive theater genre and he's very curious about the personal. He calls it, 'human-specific' but he had never worked with children and [said], "No children; it [will have] to be sweet, to be nice, it can't be dangerous." And then, because we were curious about each other's work and he wanted to work with me, I said, "That would be fantastic but I insist that it has to be a performance for children and adults. I want to prove to you that children are not a boring audience." So, that was the deal and we made one of my favorite performances.

[In *Life Live!*], we have forty audience [sic] and they came into a big, big dark room with a dark carpeted floor and six small lights hanging like little planets and they were told with a system of symbols to go to one of these planets. And around these planets, we mixed [the audience] randomly. Half the audience with children from twelve years and up and the other half were adults. The whole idea was to go on this journey together—looking at reality first, going from something that we work with a lot that we call 'Bigger reality'. [Which is] for example, if you and I realize that right now, we are sitting on a planet that is turning around 800 kilometers an hour. Just think about it. Isn't it amazing? If you go up, there is endless space on top. You can go forever. We're floating in endless space on this little planet. And this is real, right now. So, this 'Bigger reality' was just one way, one image that we did in a poetic way with music. And when the audience looks at each other and realizes that this is reality now, you feel very close [with one another]. We go all the way out and create a big image and then we go all the way in and create the smallest. "Try to find the smallest thing you can" and then everybody goes around and they come back with a little piece of dust or something and we talk about how many atoms are inside this little dust and how most of it is really emptiness and that goes for you and me as well.

So, we're doing this with reality and then the third place we're working with is the whole psychological sphere where with different games and in an abstracted way [we] look at "What do you like? What is your dislike?" [sic] "Are you afraid of dying? Are you ever thinking about the fact that you're dying one day?" [sic]. We're not afraid to go all the way because we do it in a very protected atmosphere. Of course, the question of death is one of the stronger ones and we approach that very slowly. We make all these little games where you talk about if you're shy or not; if you're brave; what you admire—we're trying to get people together to look at their whole existence, from atom level to a personal, psychological level to the whole big story. And this is all mixed with non-verbal poetic atmospheres. The only scenography we have is fifty cardboard walls that the audience are moving around together, so at some point we ask them to build a city, and they build a city however they want and it always becomes a labyrinth that you walk through and find a place to sit. And then later on they build different houses. So, the whole performance has no story, it's an exploration of reality together with these five, six, seven people that you're in a group with. That's a good representative of what we're working with now.

AK: You talked about how you have an intergenerational audience. What does an audience of younger people allow you to do that you maybe can't with adults, or vice versa? What have you noticed about those different audiences and how they respond or react or play?

STJ: There are two different things with adults and children to make them let go of themselves. With adults, the more you can make them insecure, *not* tell them what's going to happen and work with this balance of fear and curiosity. The fear can be shyness or something (but there has to be this, "Oh my God, what am I doing"), but the curiosity has to be bigger because if the fear is bigger than the curiosity, then you withdraw. You might get forced into the experience anyway, but inside, you're emotionally closed. But if the curiosity is bigger, you voluntarily take the step psychologically and for me that's the whole trick. And that works on a different level from adults than children because for adults, the more insecure you can make them, the more braver [sic] they have to be, and that's good because then they need to get out of their comfort zone. [But] with children, it tends to be that you make them feel secure. And also, the fantastic thing with children, and somebody told me this is also how they play, is that you can say, "Okay, so you're the mother and I'm the father, and this is the boat and now I'm going on the boat." [And they] don't feel that the game is ruined because we talk about it. And that's different with adults. With children, you can give them all the rules and all the frames and they can still then completely switch and then go into the fantasy of it. So, we tend to be very clear with the children about the rules, like, "In here, you cannot speak, at all. It's a quiet thing. And there are lights; you have to follow the lights. There is no story." Whatever we can say to tell them what this is.

AK: How does your work fit into the long standing history of the innovative, fearless work for children by the Danish?

STJ: In my understanding [sic], ten to fifteen years ago you had this line of hierarchy. On one end of the hierarchy, you had children's theater, and it was like you're not really an artist if you do children's theater; then in the middle, you had the commercial [theater]; and then on the other side, you had this underground theater that's very abstract and very strange and only the really weird people understand what's going on. I think I'm part of a movement that realized that if these two come together, this very abstract work over here with a very abstract audience and over here, not always but sometimes, you have a very curious, brave audience in children. And for me, that was the big revelation; if you 'get' [children] and if what you do is not intellectual but you can work with anything existential. I think that the child audience is much more abstract [than an adult audience]. I think abstraction comes before drama not dramaturgy, but before storytelling. We're abstract before we're storytellers. I would get that a lot in the beginning, "But they won't understand and there's no story," and I was like, "No, but that only happens around eight, nine years old." Then they start asking me this question, "What is it about? What is the meaning?" Because this is what they start to learn in school and in their brain things start to have to have meaning. I'm very curious about keeping that room open inside of those human beings to say, [this is] like a dream. You don't neglect the dream because you didn't understand it. Maybe it was amazing or strange or funny or scary, and if you don't understand it, it's a more interesting dream almost. So, I really like to keep that room open because in my experience we have it as children but we forget it because the world becomes all about knowing and finding the right answer. Not finding the right question.

POLYGLOT THEATRE, MELBOURNE, AUSTRALIA

Polyglot Theatre is recognized as one of Australia's leading children's theater companies and is internationally renowned as a pioneer in participatory and play-based work. The company creates two strands of performances: conceptually rich, interactive theatrical works (such as *How High the Sky* and *Separation Street*) and large-scale *"participatory art experiences for kids and families."*[9] In the former work, the company is interested in layering immersivity [sic] with more traditional spectatorship. In *How High the Sky*, there are two layers of audience and two simultaneous relationships between the audience and the performance. There is the audience of babies and one caregiver per child, who are immersed in the performance space, while at the same time there is another circle of audience on the outside looking in at the experience/performance. In *Separation Street*, adults and children go on separate immersive journeys punctuated with moments where the adult audience is allowed to peek into the children's parallel voyage.

In the Play Space Works, the entire event is the immersion into—and physical engagement with—the playing space itself and every audience participant has a cumulative physical impact on the site over the duration of the "run." *Tangle*, for example, starts as an empty space delineated by poles. Children are each given a ball of elastic string to weave around the structure in any way they wish and for over a period of days, a dense, chaotic, vibrant 'Tangle' is built. *Paper Planet* begins with

---

[9] Polyglot Theatre website, http://www.polyglot.org.au/about-us/

tall cardboard trees and the invitation to construct a world out of paper. Children and families can make anything they wish and leave it in the space contributing to the collectively built environment.

Polyglot's tag line is "*Theatre is child's play*" and it is this act of play-filled engagement that drives the work. For this company, the design and dramaturgy of the immersive form of these play space works has almost reversed back on itself to the point of near absence. The artists offer a physical, spatial or scenographic prompt, such as a thousand cardboard boxes (*We Built This City*) or the invitation and materials to make a complex labyrinth (*Sticky Maze*), but beyond that, the piece itself is completed by the audience in a communal act that takes place in real time.

Excerpts of interview with Sue Giles, Artistic Director, Polyglot Theatre:

AK: How would you describe, and how would you define the Play Space Works of Polyglot, such as *Tangle* and *Paper Planet*? Is it theater? Is it art installation? It seems to exist in a space between the two.

SG: This idea of interaction and participation, an audience becoming an embodiment of the work has been the most important thing for me in the last few years. The idea of it being theater comes up all the time. I [hear], "This is not theater, this is a playground." And one of the most important things for us, as creators, is that it actually retains a lot of the theatrical elements that makes it different to a playground. And part of that is about ritual…and an audience's commitment to a piece; and the idea that things can happen within it that have drama, that take you outside your everyday experience; and that we create a different world each time that these things are created too. But ultimately, the element that is vital for all of these works is the audience itself. In a way, we don't ever know how it's going to roll out until that audience engages.

AK: What does the term *immersive* mean to you in this context of your work?

SG: *Immersive* feels to me that you are embedded in the thing. I often talk about the kind of theater that I create [as] experiential theater. Theater through doing, theater through being in it. That takes me down an interesting path when thinking about this stuff. Because when it comes to children, their idea of immersive experience is completely different to an adult's idea of this. And the same with participation and…with interaction. And that I think is the key to this. A [child's] understanding of these things and what they bring to an audience body provides an enormous adventure for the theater maker. And so, I understand *immersive* as being something that engages all the senses, that you feel physically involved in it, as well as involved emotionally.

AK: Do children respond differently than adults to immersive and participatory work?

SG: The first time I ever made this sort of work was in response to my own children's experience of play in the backyard with a cardboard box. So, the first work I ever made was thousands of cardboard boxes in a big construction site. It's called We Built

This City. It's still going. It's been going for fifteen years now. That sort of work came from this idea that imagination [and] imaginative play only needs very, very simple things to thrive. And my desire was to create an empty palette, if you like, go back to the basics, to a string and a stick, and see what you can make from that. It's almost like reinventing boredom as well, and boredom is an incredibly creative tool. So, observing how kids then reacted to that, that empty palette, the blank sheet of paper, that was the inspiration for absolutely everything else after that. What I've observed was…that less is more…The kids took the opportunity and ran with it. And every time somebody has wanted to make it more…you could say more complex, but I don't believe that's true, more narrative based, I've struggled to keep it as simple as possible…part of the way that kids engage is complete involvement in imaginative play. That's their secret power. Their ability to jump from one solution to another; their ability to have divergent thinking around a particular problem; to go from one world to the next within the space of a minute…this was a chance for me to see how the routine and the knowledge and the habits and the huge story background that adults have after they've grown up, actually didn't do the play any service at all. The kids, through their kind of ignorance of all of that, are making the biggest leaps and making the greatest groundbreaking offers, and this has been true for all the processes that we use in creating work.

AK: If the immersive experiences you are making for children are, as you say, deliberately open or somewhat of a blank slate, how do you modify that for an adult audience? Or do you?

SG: We just finished making a new work this year, *Separation Street*, which took adults and children on very separate journeys around the same story…when we were creating the adult journey, we felt like we had to fill the whole thing in because they needed to be supported for the entire journey, otherwise they'd feel embarrassed, at a loss, they'd start to question, they would feel grumpy, they'd wish there was a bar…and then with the kids, our challenge was to completely leave an open space. And so, we gave them an incredibly abstract journey and that was just filled with lights and sound and image. And even then, the images were very, very abstract. At one point, we just put fifteen tents in a room and just saw what they did with it. And that was enough. There was this entire world created just through their own imaginative play. Whereas, the adults, we had to pamper them through the thing, and every now and then they get to see the kids at play; [we] allow them a window onto what the possibilities were once for them.

It's a really interesting thing with Punchdrunk's work [for example]—the detail is immense, and so you're constantly looking for meaning and constantly trying to follow the narrative. For an adult, that's an incredibly compelling journey. The difference then with the children is that [they] live in it and breathe it…I always talk about the adults and kids in parallel universes. It's so funny that we completely forget how that universe operates. And that's kind of glorious. Because if you become aware of it and become aware of how differently they see the world and what a different perspective they can then bring to whatever you create, that's a huge power I reckon.

AK: Who else is making immersive, audience-centric; audience-reliant work in this way, either for young people or adults? Are you the only one in the world doing this?

SG: That's a really interesting question, because I think we might be!...there are all sorts of different and really exciting participatory and immersive things going on. There are a lot of beautiful interactive playground stuff and amazing live art that gets created. But I think the idea of performance and theater as the driver in these big scale works is quite unusual...the idea of us creating a world in which people make and stay and play. They actually create the world that then becomes the common playground and the common work of art. That's quite unique actually.

AK: Could you talk more about this communal aspect of the work? And how the duration of a piece plays into that?

SG: I think this is a really interesting because you get this kind of a collegiate commitment from the audience that participates: it's theirs...people are actually making it. And when they make it, they want to see that it's going be okay or they want to see it as it grows. It's quite a beautiful human characteristic actually. And also, the changes. And we've had trouble in that way too because some children will come back to *Paper Planet* and what they created isn't there anymore. It's been changed or it's been moved or someone's turned it into something else, so there's danger in that commitment as well. With something like *Tangle*...it needs to be up for three days or else it just isn't as fat and glorious and insane as it possibly can be. And some of them do exist for one day only. *We Built This City* can exist for one day only. And it has worked that way several times. But because that is constantly evolving and it gets knocked down all the time and it gets rebuilt all the time, it has its own time-lapse history in some way. I love seeing an audience walking away, looking behind them and going, "we made that." And there's something incredibly satisfying about leaving your mark on a city or on a space in that way, especially if you're a child...I believe that these experiences [have] the potential for great impact, they've got a great potential for bridging that gap between adults and children. And that's kind of one of the big charms of it, I think.

AK: So, this isn't just for the kids, this is somehow a communion, a bridging across ages?

SG: That's my not-so-secret agenda through absolutely all the work that I create. All the stuff that we make is an opportunity for adults to see children through different eyes for a minute. We rarely see our kids at a distance. We don't get to see them being physically strong or courageous, we don't see them make their own choices. These are the things that we'd love them to do but...sometimes don't have the space, the power, the chance, the ability to actually let them make these things...so I guess this is kind of our reaction to an over protectiveness of children with the result that they're not deemed capable people. And actually, all of these spaces prove the capability of children for what they have. Not because they're small adults growing up, because they are kids who have special powers. And I think these special powers all become very visible [and] adults can see them in action. *Separation Street* is a perfect example of a piece of theater where they literally saw through a two-way mirror children playing in secret, and the adults had sort of an "Oh!" moment...so yes, the agenda through all of this is for adults to see the kind of power and capability of children when they are able to make their own choices and they are responsible for their own actions.

It all comes down to this idea of choice and freedom and it's interesting too for me that a child's perspective on both those things are again very different to an adult's. I think that's the thing that all of these works examine really strongly. Freedom for an adult means one thing...and kids who experienced freedom when it was given to them...didn't experience it as having to do with responsibility...it's like the kids' idea of freedom was, "no-one's gonna tell us what to do, woo hoo! We're free. We can bash stuff up!" You know? First time we tried it, they did. They went to town. I think the idea of freedom is a central part of what we're exploring and the idea that the individual desire can be completely influenced by the community that they're in. One of the great things that *Tangle* does for me in terms of the greater context for children in the world is that each individual child with their individual line then becomes completely crisscrossed with everybody else's and the only way that play can begin is when everybody's involved. Their freedom is reliant on other people.

CHAPTER 2

Site and Seduction: Space, Sensuality, and Use-Value in the Immersive Theater

Paul Masters

Imagine that you enter a parlor. You come late. When you arrive, others have long preceded you, and they are engaged in a heated discussion, a discussion too heated for them to pause and tell you exactly what it is about. In fact, the discussion began long before any of them got there, so that no one present is qualified to retrace for you all the steps that had gone before. You listen for a while, until you decide that you have caught the tenor of the argument; then you put in your oar. Someone answers; you answer him; another comes to your defense; another aligns himself against you, to either the embarrassment or gratification of your opponent, depending on the quality of your ally's assistance. However, the discussion is interminable. The hour grows late, you must depart. And you do depart, with the discussion still vigorously in progress.[10]

At a nondescript doorway on Forty-sixth street, an unusual queue forms. Men sport three piece suits, bowties, and dinner jackets. Ladies, not to be outdone, glitter in an array of designer dresses, jewelry, and sequins. Passersby stare at us: are we an undercover movie premiere? An odd bit of performance art? Just eccentric New Yorkers? Not quite. We have been instructed to dress "to please the queen" for a spectacle known as *The Queen of the Night* (2013).[11] Produced in part by Randy Weiner, a New York City theatre veteran known for *The Donkey Show* (New York City, 1999, Boston, 2008), *Sleep No More* (New York City, 2014), and vaudeville-supper club The Box (New York City, 2008), I have been prepared to expect over-the-top extravagance. The space's moniker is promising—Queen of the Night runs in a space known as The Diamond Horseshoe. The former site of a nightclub opened by theatre impresario Billy Rose in 1938, it currently lies underneath Midtown's Paramount Hotel. After a multimillion dollar renovation, the long-dormant club has now been reopened for what promises to be a spectacular affair.

The blank door finally opens, and we file down an unremarkable white hallway. Leaving the street behind, eager patrons shuffle in out of the cold to check purses and overcoats. Another white hallway follows. So far, the surroundings are bare-contrasting starkly with the high drama and pitch dark entry of *Sleep No More's* (2008, 2010) or *Then She Fell's* (2012, 2013) prop-heavy medical waiting room.

---

[10] Burke, Kenneth. The Philosophy of Literary Form (Baton Rouge: Louisiana State University Press, 1967), 110–111.

[11] E-mail communication from The Queen of The Night (5 May 2014).

Suddenly, we find ourselves at the top of a stunning art-deco stairwell, gleaming white and softly curved. Participants seem to float down the well-worn treads, deep into the bowels of a city many thought they already knew. Stacks of champagne glasses are stacked haphazardly in the first landing, alluding perhaps to the raucous celebrations of Billy Rose's heyday. Here as well attendants in halter-top tuxedos and short black breeches (designed by couturier Thom Browne) greet us with silver trays full of cocktails.[12] Mine tastes of gin and smoke, rosemary and bitters. Our descent continues another flight. We finally reach the bottom of the staircase. Here we wait expectantly, sipping our drinks as other patrons file in behind us.

Gilt frames and marble floors sparkle in the half-light of a lobby or antechamber. To my left, red velvet curtains conceal openings in the wall. Directly across from the stairs, a glass partition exposes a bare-breasted woman on a revolving platform. The audience murmurs, wondering aloud whether or not the delicately spangled, still figure is a mannequin. She begins to move slowly, sinuously. She bears a crown on her head—could this be the titular Queen? In a few moments, more black-and-white attired company members stream out from the velvet clad opening and begin grabbing audience members indiscriminately, leading the way across the small lobby and through the curtains.

One of the many attractive performers grabs the end of my tie, leading me, not too softly, toward what seems to be a backstage area. There, in a dimly lit space filled with stage ropes and cables, another company member meets us. He has pulled another participant away from the crowded entry hall. We take shots of an unknown liquid, poured from a tap hidden by more damask curtains. We make a toast. My attractive guide grabs my tie again, loosening it, and unfastening the top button of my shirt. Nodding approvingly at her handiwork, she tells me to "be good" tonight, but not "too good." Abruptly, I am ejected from the backstage area through a curtain. I find myself standing on a stage.

The ballroom is an oval with burnished tile on the walls, elegant archways framing openings on each side, and banquettes lining the two long sides in soft curves. Lights glitter off of polished surfaces and from behind curtains. Soft ovals appear everywhere in the design, from the gilt and stucco detail to the wrought-iron handrails. It is an overwhelming first impression. I walk down from the stage on a wide, steep set of stairs—this is a small proscenium on a short end of the oval. It is full of chairs, stacked crazily, as if another party had just left in a hurry. At the other end a long bar, shining and curved, dominates the space. In between, bare tables and iron barricades are arranged to keep audience from crossing the floor. Instead we are allowed to move towards the bar through side passages extending the length of the rectangle. As people continue to enter, several areas are lit to reveal acrobats performing a variety of sensuous, highly athletic, dances on tables and platforms. The scene feels familiar, yet strange—a ballroom lost in time, rediscovered and relit with the extravagant glitz of Broadway.

Repurposing non-traditional or disused spaces for performance events, immersive theatres make use of a prototypical theatrical practice. From the renovation of an auto garage by Richard Schechner and his Performance Group in the 1960s, to site-specific performances created by Mike Pearson and Brith Gof in the 1980s, non-

---

[12] Thom Browne is an American fashion designer.

traditional sites and spaces have been critical to performance for decades. In *immersive* theatre, however, emphasis on the real-time sensual engagement of participants alters the relationship of spaces to theatrical events. Spaces in these scenarios become vessels for sights, sounds, smells, and tastes that imbue abstract, sometimes surreal surroundings with concrete and powerful immediacy. These transformations reimagine the relationship of the theatrical site, or ground, to other material and bodily aspects of the theatre.

As the vocabulary of theatrical technology has expanded over the past two decades, immersive theatre has accumulated spatial and aesthetic formats designed to bridge the gap between presence and mediation, space and time. Appropriating the jargon of digital media, the term promises spatial and sensual experiences beyond any encountered in new media alone. For these performance events, the live, visceral quality of theatre makes the sensual impact of immersion possible. And because immersion, as a label, has become indicative of both a type of experience and a trending brand, it reveals itself through a broad range of aesthetic and branded impulses. In these circumstances, site becomes a powerful asset. Abandoned schools, parking lots, and apartment blocks have become highly popular grounds for immersive events.

Foregrounding use-value, agency, and sociopolitical contexts through the lens of a participant, I define a continuum of immersive projects in this chapter. First, there are self-styled immersions, concentrated on a narrowly defined spectrum of participatory and sensual experiences. On the other, lie those events that, by dint of aesthetic and sensual languages, manifest all the markers of immersion without the branding impulses—immersive events that prove inclusive of social and political engagement with relation to site and site-use. In reviewing the gamut of corporal sites in immersive theatre, I also review the expansion of site via the advent of digital spaces, participation, and activities that stimulate, provoke, and control the act of performance.

A wide range of events has been labeled immersive, so-called either by the companies themselves or by the media that covers them. As such, *Queen of the Night* represents the most narrowly defined of the four productions discussed in this dissertation, a self-proclaimed immersive spectacle that concentrates on the solicitation and containment of individual sensuality and sexuality. Third Rail Project's *Then She Fell* negotiates a middle ground approach between authority and agency, pure voyeurism and self-reflection. In the production's Kingsland Ward, participants have intimate interactions with actors (as noted above, there are only fifteen audience members per production), as well as appreciable time to negotiate the impact of physical site without mediation. *Speakeasy Dollhouse* (2011), an event that takes place in the context of a former speakeasy, also utilizes a combination of spatial agency and control, urging participants to play an investigative role in the drama. Finally, Mike Pearson's work with Brith Gof never utilizes the language of immersion, but maintains sensitivity to social, sensual, and political contexts through such pieces as *Goddodin* (1988). *Goddodin*, along with Mike Pearson's important contributions to dramaturgical theory and practice, recognizes and excavates a methodology for socially engaged site-use—one that produces a fusion of both *virtual* and reconstructed histories that could be used in contemporary performance events. Through this range of immersions, complex patterns with regard to space emerge, problematizing current configurations of site, use, and participation in the current theatrical environment of New York City.

I argue in this chapter that immersive sites are, more often than not, removed from their communal and sociopolitical histories in the interest of creating immersive performances. Instead, as with productions such as *Queen of the Night* and *Then She Fell*, alternate, virtual histories are fabricated for immersive performances that suit the terms devised by the production. Furthermore, the creation and marketing of these virtual histories transform an audience's expectations of performance; manufacturing and bounding desires that, more often than not, will remain unsatisfied in the moment of performance. Lastly, I assert that the former three activities—isolating site from history, manufacturing and marketing desires, and fabricating virtual histories, all provocatively connect to models of technological space, e.g. hypertexts, interconnectivity, the boundaries, and negotiation of virtual environments.

Immersive aesthetics, with their emphasis on the sensate experiences of the body, transform the relationship of site to ideologies and sociocultural histories. Since *immersion*, broadly, removes participants to an alternate, all-encompassing reality, it divorces audiences from public, political, engagements that remain incumbent upon traditional theatrical forms. Whereas in the darkened auditorium audiences remain acutely aware of the performance as separated from their daily lives, immersive formats attempt to sever, or at least blur, the relationship between reality and performance, virtual time and real time. As such, aspects of *immersion* transform space into sensory, multidimensional worlds, exhibiting a tendency to ignore the specificity of social contexts involved in the choosing, inhabiting, or reviving of particular spaces. Lyn Gardner, writing for *The Guardian*, writes about Punchdrunk Theatre Company and its use of site:

Katie Spain at Grassroots was "moved [by Punchdrunk's *Faust*] in such a way that my insides were squirming, my brain twisting in fear and delight." The use of space is inspired, the experience heightened by its unfamiliarity, and Hazel at Londonist has noticed a trend: "Site-specific art and performances are all the rage at the moment," she writes. Hazel was talking about London, but I wonder whether this is a nationwide phenomenon.

Hazel also wonders whether development for the Olympics in 2012 might lead to a dearth of such derelict spaces. "Artists have responded by grabbing hold of what we've got now...before it all goes away." I suspect London, like most cities, will always have abandoned spaces; and one can't really argue against the development of affordable housing so that we can still enjoy these as they are. But it is great that people are exploiting them—and not, in the interests of balance, just for raves. Punchdrunk are dedicated to site-specific theatre and have already made use of a former distillery in Deptford for an interpretation of *The Tempest* and a former Geological Survey building in Exeter for *The Cherry Orchard*. I will certainly go to whatever they create next.[13]

Exploiting site, these London productions expose complex social problems relating to space. This is especially true of the struggle for affordable housing in the midst a trending "rage" for site-specific and immersive theatrical experiences. In this

[13] Gardner, Lyn. "The Play's Location's The Thing," The Guardian, 9 March 2007. *http://www.theguardian.com/stage/theatreblog/2007/ mar/09/*theplayslocationsthething.

case, the negotiation between site and social context relates to aspects of economics, gentrification, and the fate of fragile historical sites in urban space. Stripped of their former identity and laden with expectation, immersion elides these problems to create what I call *constructed history*. By *constructed history*, I mean an imagined history created solely by, and for, a given performance.

Constructed history, as a method of structuring space and spatial interactions, engages the audience in a legacy, a historical frame establishing heightened stakes in the corporal performance event. For *Queen of the Night*, this means translating the sensual impact of pre-war Broadway into the context of pre-recession American wealth. For *Sleep No More*, the derelict warehouses of Chelsea become the McKittrick Hotel, and for *Then She Fell*, a former parochial school becomes Kingsland Ward, a nineteenth-century asylum. In each of these instantiations, the ground of performance becomes resituated in a constructed history—a history that appears to extend both backwards and forwards in time, becoming so enmeshed in the theatrical ground that no other narrative maintains coherence. By extension, the *constructed history* created for immersive performances disconnects sites from their concrete historicity, alienating participants from the social context of the event's geography. Constructing an alternate historical narrative in lieu of the event-proper requires, as discussed further below, the maintenance and curation of a world that appears and feels *immersive*—a vibrant, unified, and viscerally present landscape.

Films, and especially the horror genre, have taken advantage of this methodology for some time. Two examples illustrate the sorts of *virtual histories* appropriated by the immersive theatre particularly well: 1999's *Blair Witch Project* and 2002's *The Ring*. *The Blair Witch Project* took advantage of the then-emerging technology of the Internet to publicize a fictional found-film "documentary." Three students hike into the Maryland wilderness to find out what became of the notorious Blair Witch, only to go missing like her other victims. Their film is supposedly found in the wilderness—the only sign of the students that authorities are able to uncover. The film's use of the Internet for publicity purposes became an early example of viral advertisement, and the historical backstory created for the film proved highly credible to audiences. *Entertainment Weekly* wrote that "When *The Blair Witch Project* came out in 1999, some people thought the film was true: "They thought these three kids really went into the woods and disappeared forever, leaving only their video cameras full of spooky footage behind."[14] Partly, this virtual historiography succeeded because of the detail involved in the film's "timeline" of events stretching from 1785–1995 (1995 is the year the film was supposedly found).[15] Additionally, few publicity messages relayed explicitly that the film was fictional, introducing further ambivalence into the viewing experience. Whether or not audiences believed or disbelieved, the wholly fabricated history left an indelible mark on the subgenre of found-film horror.

Similarly, the immersive production *Speakeasy Dollhouse* (2011) also claims to be based on real events. Documents related to a mob hit in the Lower East Side of Manhattan appear on the production's website. These also appear in e-mails sent to

---

[14] Bacle, Ariana. "'Blair Witch Project' actors talk going hungry on set," Entertainment Weekly, 6 October 2014. *http://www.ew.com/article /2014/* 10/06/blair-witch-project-found-footage.

[15] http://www.blairwitch.com/mythology.html.

audiences before attendance at the performance. A Blogger site full of photographs, letters, and other ephemera related to the crime are left for participants to pore through like private investigators.[16] Upon entering the speakeasy bar (also located in the Lower East Side), participants receive investigative roles to play throughout the evening. The virtual, archival world bleeds into the space of the viscerally present, crowded bar. As with *The Blair Witch Project*, where the veracity of historical events leads into a perceptual reorganization of the film's viewing, *Speakeasy Dollhouse's* flirtation with the archive prepares audiences to participate fully, establishing a priori principles for negotiating the space of performance.

2002's *The Ring* presents another such example. *The Blair Witch Project* aspired to deepen and expand the experience of the film through its media campaign, but *The Ring* aspired to viral status through the dissemination of a fictional, viral film seen within *The Ring*—a film within a film. These metatheatrics played into the films' broader plot, namely one concerning the viewing of a supernatural VHS tape that inevitably causes the viewer's death seven days later. The film, as cultural critique, mirrors anxieties concerning new and emergent technologies (i.e. widely available viral films), using a format (VHS) that was already disappearing when the film was made. Beyond this "film-within-a-film" device, the website devised a further mythology for the supernatural characters, mostly involving the usual suspects associated with the horror genre: a creepy old house, an abandoned farm, an insane asylum, and a demonic child.[17]

Then She Fell also provides an asylum to house its part-biographical, part-fictional approach to Lewis Carrol and his works. Filling in historical gaps left about the nature of Carrol's relationship with his muse, Alice Liddell, the performance interweaves the whimsical literature of the Alice tales with the dark, sometimes brooding sadness of Carrol's life. Like *The Ring*, where the mythological history of the film's antagonists provides an extension and completion of the plot, *Then She Fell* manufactures an asylum in order to color and enliven the historical and imaginative framework of Carrol's life. The choice of an asylum also offers up a familiar trope to participants. The asylum is a place for strangeness and the throwing-off of imaginative constraints. *Then She Fell's* title alludes directly to the asylum-space. Signifying Alice's rabbit-hole (what she fell in to in *Alice in Wonderland*), as well as her real-life separation from Carrol, the asylum becomes simultaneously a place of control and wildness, inhibition and imagination. Such dualities occur in many of the aesthetic assemblages of the immersive theatre. The wholesale creation of such histories reinterprets the space-time of the performance event, augmenting and extending its presence beyond the walled environs of sites themselves.

In the sense that these *virtual histories* often become indistinguishable from real circumstances, the sites of immersive performance observed here also engage, willingly or not, in the sociopolitical ideology of neoliberalism. Participatory and visceral, yet highly stratified and artificial, immersive theatres maintain a focus on the experiential nature of space as well as the creation of alternative, fictional histories. Invariably, relegating the social, public, context of sites to *virtual* narratives and sensual experiences reinforces ideological structures mirrored in the technologies and

---

[16] Speakeasy Dollhouse. *http://speakeasydollhouseevidence.* blogspot.com
[17] The Ring. http://thering.asmik-ace.co.jp/.

sociopolitical culture of the free market. Something here about how the above implicates many immersive theatres—in that they support the view promoted by neoliberalism—that the individual could maintain agency within growing disparities in wealth, access to social resources, and labor.[18]

Immersive theatres, with their promise of autonomy and agency in imaginary realities, often put the onus on individuals to create their own narrative of a production. Yet, as observed in prior discussions, pushing the boundaries of these performances often results in confrontations with constraints and structures that delimit both the activity of participants and the potential narratives available in each performance event.[19] Agency and autonomy, along with site and context, branding and reality, are blurred by the imagery and power of spatial and temporal forces in the *immersive* theatre. This blurring, coupled by the creation of aesthetic and pseudohistorical homogeneity both pre- and post-production, parallels the neoliberal elision of inclusive social narratives.

Critical to the *neoliberal* structures latent in *immersion*, theatre companies also layer the physical act of performance with a potent mix of technology and new media. Observable in both film and theatre, these often support a hierarchical, authoritative approach to historical narratives, creating what heretofore has been defined as *constructed history*, be that of a site, body or text. With its cultural cache and overwhelming prevalence, social technologies allow performances to take place in partially, or entirely, mediated environments. In the case of the performances discussed here, pre-performance communications prepare participants to engage in specific activities during the real-time event, establish spatial/performance boundaries, and control the narrative meanings available to participants. Expanding the concepts of site and performance beyond the typical, real-time boundaries of events, immersion realizes a bewildering variety of virtual spaces running parallel to the event-proper. These spaces radiate beyond tangible, corporal forms and into a variety of mediated and participatory experiences that can occur before, during, and after the performance. Taking the form of e-mails, mobile applications, websites, archival material, blogs, texts, photographs, and many others, these augmentations become an important part of the spatial arrangements of immersion.[20]

Not to be confused with theatrical ephemera such as playbills, posters, photographs, or even set dressings, websites and other virtual media often enhance and expand performance events, playing a role in the provocation of desire, curiosity, and expectations integral to the structure of the immersive world. Websites, in our digital world, never die. Even stored sites from the birth of the Internet are still available for the nostalgic to peruse. This is true of Third Rail Project's *Then She Fell* (2012, 2013), a performance where the texts of Lewis Carroll prepare participants for the topsy-turvy world of the asylum in which the event takes place. The production's associated website describes a range of participatory/sensory experiences that mirror structural aspects of the event. Similarly, *Speakeasy Dollhouse* (2011) begins with e-

---

[18] See Chapter 2 for more discussions of neoliberalism in the immersive theatre, esp. via Claire Bishop's *Artificial Hells* (Verso, 2012). Her work, which focuses on participation, notes that "In this logic [of neoliberalism] participation in society is merely participation in the task of being individually responsible for what, in the past, was the collective concern of the state" (14).

[19] Chapter 2 especially relates several run-ins with the boundaries of immersive events.

[20] Each of the productions discussed in this dissertation engage in one or more of these practices.

mailed documentation of an unsolved mob-hit in Manhattan's Lower East Side. These e-mails ask participants to become investigators of a sort, engaging them in the context of the space's reality long before entry into the speakeasy. In both these instances, the space-time of performance expands to include parallel activities in virtual spaces—spaces that articulate and bound the potential for participation, agency, and sensuality in a given event.

Queen of the Night's corporal and virtual spaces revolve around the now-legendary Billy Rose. Rose, whose penchant for the spectacular lives on in the Diamond Horseshoe's reimagined space, was no foreigner to creating theatrical spectacles. Through a series of business ventures in theatres, nightclubs, and music halls through the early 1950s, he left a legacy that still impacts the New York City theatre scene.[21] *Vanity Fair,* whose fifth anniversary celebration took place in the original Horseshoe in 1988, heralded the public reopening of the ballroom in 2014 with an article highlighting Rose's outsized personality:

> Billy Rose opened the Diamond Horseshoe for the first time on Christmas, in 1938. Rose had already masterminded Jumbo, an elaborate circus-themed musical, and nightspots like the Billy Rose Music Hall, whose hallmarks were a hearty dose of nostalgia, spiced with Rose's own outlandish bravura. At the Diamond Horseshoe, he conjured a Gay Nineties-themed saloon: the walls of the main room were painted deep red and white with period fixtures, while the staircase was plastered with posters of bygone vaudeville stars.[22]

For the America of 1938—a nation on the brink of war and still in the grip of the Great Depression—the Horseshoe's escapist theme proved successful. *Queen of the Night* follows a similarly troubled era of American history: post-war and post-recession, the ballroom's lavish decorations gaze wistfully back to the heady days before the 2006 financial crisis. Following Billy Rose's strategy of nostalgic escapism, the production uses the Diamond Horseshoe to generate and authorize, through a reimagining of Billy Rose's aesthetic, a variation of immersive theatre that offers sex, excess, and indulgence—for a price. And, while *Queen of the Night* creates a similar environment as other so-called immersive events—with its art-installed space, freedom to wander, and chance encounters with actors—the production curtails the agency these events often provide to participants. Synthesizing the sit-down format of Rose's club with the promise of spectacle (acrobatics, nudity, and the possibility of intimate contact), the physical and virtual spaces of the performance enforce

---

[21] Cambridge Guide to Theatre "Rose, Billy": "his ventures ranged from nightclubs and theatre-restaurants (Back Stage Club, Casino de Paree, the Billy Rose Music Hall in New York during the 1920s and 30s; Casa Mañana in Fort Worth in the 1930s; New York's Diamond Horseshoe, 1939–52) to epic spectacles such as Jumbo (1945) and the aquacades at the 1939–40 New York World's Fair and the San Francisco Golden Gate Exposition (1940), as well as 11 legitimate Broadway productions, including Carmen Jones (1943) and The Immoralist (1954). In the 1950s and 60s he owned two New York theatres. Among Rose's five marriages was one to Fanny Brice (1929). The Billy Rose Theatre Collection of the New York Public Library was funded by his foundation (organized in 1958)."

[22] Monahan, Patrick, "The Diamond Horseshoe, the World War II-Era Nightclub Resurrected by Randy Weiner and Simon Hammerstein," Vanity Fair. January 24, 2014. Accessed August 2, 2014, http://www.vanityfair.com/online/daily/2014/01/diamond-horseshoe-nightclub-simon-hammerstein.

restrictive mores. These mores strip away the necessity of narrative in exchange for desires that remain, for the most part, unfulfilled.

Queen of the Night's move towards non-narrative theatrical immersion proves atypical in the New York City theatre scene. In Punchdrunk's *Sleep No More* (2009, 2012) or Third Rail Project's *Then She Fell*, (2013, 2014) patrons negotiate the nuances of spaces and bodies to craft meanings enhanced or augmented by props and performers. *Queen of the Night*, by contrast, deemphasizes narrative construction in favor of sensuality alone. While this dinner-theatre/floor show/bacchanal replicates, interpretively, an image of the Diamond Horseshoe's original goings-on under Rose's ownership, the commercial interests of the performance lie more in providing a constant and overwhelming flow of sensory stimuli than a historical reconstruction. Effectively removing participants' agency to construct narratives for themselves— consumption, conspicuous and otherwise, becomes the primary mode of participation. Harnessing the Horseshoe's history, exclusivity and social hierarchy emerge, as with the original Diamond Horseshoe, from nostalgia for the recent past.

Figure 1: Queen's Club

Nostalgia, history, and memory, in turn, all play a role in the creation of *Queen of the Night's* theatre-space; a landscape created in both concrete and virtual spheres. While the Diamond Horseshoe's renovation capitalizes on Billy Rose's aesthetic strategies, the virtual spaces created by the production's branding on its website, e-mails, external blogs, and press, enhances the Horseshoe's stylish, jet-setting image, setting expectations for the evening that outstrip the performance's potential experiences. As with other *immersive* events, the managing and manipulation of the event pre-performance primes participants for entry into the site. However, *Queen of the Night* takes this agenda one step further, creating a sense of exclusivity through costly, value-added experiences. *Sleep No More* pioneered this concept in the New

York City theatre scene through an increasingly diverse set of spaces that includes two bars (Mandalay and The Gallows Green) and now a restaurant (The Heath). Access to these venues is not contingent on attendance at the performance. In *Queen of the Night*, the add-on experiences become part of the production: you need a ticket to experience them. Additionally, such experiences relate to the potential stimulation participants might be privy to—sexual or otherwise. As examples, Figures 1 and 2 provide typical e-mail communications about *Queen of the Night's* extra-curricular events. Figure 1 advertises access to the *Queen's Club*, a free-membership club that keeps the party going long after the performance has officially ended. The image of a slender woman in a chastity belt alludes to the type of naughty, sexy play that might transpire "after the show" when "the party continues" into the small hours. The advertisement also comes straight to the point, putting legs and crotch front-and-center in the frame. Bare midriff and all, the image leaves little to be imagined, but much to be desired—a desire that proves critical to *Queen of the Night's* branding. However, whereas the image in Figure 1 focuses the composition of the e-mail on legs and crotch, the text of Figure 2 provokes a similarly titillating, transparent, message of seduction.

The message of Figure 2, "Lose Inhibitions, Make Resolutions," contrasts with my own experience of the production, where at least one patron was ejected for losing more of his inhibitions than was deemed appropriate.[23] No surprise then that this image appears to tell two different stories. First, the text at the top catches the eye, inspiring a reaction not unlike Figure 1's legs. However, the restrained elegance of the image, the statuesque font, and the floral motif bring the eyes down to "Black-Tie Masquerade Gala." "Black-tie" implies elegance, exclusivity, a sense of decorum, and perhaps even restraint. The Queen herself appears offset, regal and demure—far from the bare-breasted and spectacularly decorated Queen greeting participants in the Horseshoe's lobby.

---

[23] At my experience of the production, a man got drunk and tried to reach for the titular Queen's bare legs.

Figure 2: Queen of the Night

Both Figures 1 and 2 have similarities to advertisements, which is in fact what they are, but this direct branding through sexually explicit language and imagery proves significantly different than the tactics employed by either *Sleep No More* or *Then She Fell*. In these latter productions, the emphasis on curiosity, intimacy, and discovery in the context of the physical site characterizes the performance as a mystery, a labyrinth for individuals to traverse. In *Queen of the Night*, the language and imagery has been stripped down to the desire for both access and sexual release. In neither case does the production afford individual participants the former without proper real-world credentials: i.e. cash.

Explicitly setting out rules and expectations for interaction in the physical space of the Diamond Horseshoe, these images also tender implicit, subtly manipulated messaging. The sexual tone obscures the subtext involved, while also playing a role in defining the immersive space. Returning to the concept of *constructed history*, these types of images prove critical to crafting the Diamond Horseshoe's narrative as revived theatre-site, as well as establishing aesthetic continuity with what participants will see upon entering the ballroom's glittering oval. However, the messages sent by these e-mails also suggest dissonant impulses. On the one hand, Figure 1 appears to promise sexual revelry, but does so in the guise of a woman in a chastity belt, and on the other, Figure 2 provides a restrained image coupled with enticing language. This play of image and language leaves prospective participants with semiotic confusion—a confusion that appreciably increases the production's flirtatious attitude with its guests. In addition, both figures establish the site's permanence over time. Through a neo-Rococo aesthetic, the e-mails invite entry into an elegant and luxurious club atmosphere, suggesting both intimacy and exclusivity. By appropriating a historical, decorative approach, the pieces also suggest a sense of history and lineage that authorizes the promised excesses of the "Queen's Club" and "Masquerade Gala." The *constructed history* of the Horseshoe, overall, intimates a site in which excess and glamour are tempered with rules and decorous elegance.

These e-mails, along with other communications about the production, prioritize desire and sensation above narrative or participation. If a narrative existed, it might be best expressed by the words uttered to me upon entering the Horseshoe—"be good" but not "too good." With this interaction in mind, *Queen of the Night* again contrasts with several other *immersive* productions. *Sleep No More; Then She Fell*; and *Speakeasy Dollhouse* all utilize textual narrative as a major component of their experiences. For this reason, *Queen of the Night* models *immersion* as a term of cultural production, and exhibits the strongest evidence that aesthetic or sensual *immersion* exists in distinction from commercial or branded *immersion*. *Queen of the Night*, through its construction of excess and trompe l'oeil spectacle, illuminates the entanglements between these two formats. As such, the Diamond Horseshoe's renewed popularity highlights and problematizes aspects of immersion latent in other site-engaged experiences. The necessity of the individual actor-participant to be self-sustaining, to translate the (often dissonant) impulses of the productions' virtual and physical spaces on his or her own, and to adjust to the rules deployed pro-or retro-actively into the performance landscape, deemphasizes linear space-time in favor of a one-size-fits all performance philosophy—one that simultaneously expects participants to produce their own narratives in space while limiting their ability to do so.

Whereas virtual spaces, new media, and found spaces all play a role in the construction of immersive sites, so too do macro practices that structure the experiences inside immersive events. The specific uses of performance sites also raise questions concerning the social and political ramifications of such spaces and how they absorb or interpolate aesthetic and commercial technologies. *Queen of the Night's* e-mails provide a clear example of how this branding works in the virtual world; aesthetics and commercialism intertwine to create an immersive brand as much as sensory experiences in concrete spaces. While use varies based on the context of each production, the emphasis on site as an atmospheric, sensual, and image-laden interactive experience holds true in many immersive events.

Immersive theatre's use of site attempts to liberate it from the textuality of modern drama, using site to construct ephemeral landscapes that take the place of text. In the sense that immersion represents a broader social attention to images, sites, and interactivity, it appears corollary to a broader techno-cultural shift. Indeed, the aspects of immersion that parallels video/virtual reality games as whole-cloth constructions, taking place more and more immersively, challenges any one definition of the theatrical practice(s) purportedly being discussed here. Hans-Thies Lehmann's influential work *Post Dramatic Theatre* (2006) expresses some of the problems produced by the classification of *immersion* succinctly:

In the face of the pressure created by the united forces of speed and surface, theatrical discourse emancipates itself from literary discourse but at the same time draws nearer to it in terms of its general function within culture. For both theatre and literature are textures which are especially dependent on the release of active energies of imagination, energies that are becoming weaker in a civilization of the primarily passive consumption of images and data...theatre means the collectively spent and used up lifetime in the collectively breathed air of that space in which the performing and spectating take place...Its profoundly changed mode of theatrical sign usage suggests that it makes sense to describe a significant sector of the new theatre as "post dramatic." [Emphasis added][24]

Lehmann's analysis of the cultural moment refines the boundaries of site in immersion. "Speed and surface" have shifted the aims of theatre and literature, with the "passive consumption of images" taking their place. Synthesizing images, sites, and new media forms to establish the structure and bounds of immersive environments, productions maintain order through the organization of time and space rather than bodies or texts. *Queen of the Night*, for example, depends on the Diamond Horseshoe's past grandeur to enable its aesthetic and commercial excesses. *Sleep No More* and *Then She Fell* in turn utilize painstakingly detailed installations to fragment and refract canonical texts. In these productions, imagistic and spatial aesthetics take precedence over the live presence of bodies, spoken words, or spontaneous imaginings.

Then She Fell, whose Kingsland Ward asylum removes participants to an unknown point in Lewis Carroll's nineteenth century, reproduces the signal manipulation of space and time described in part by Lehmann. Starting in a waiting room filled to the brim with books, medical files, and a giant desk, participants go on to experience a sequence of rooms and interactions particular to each individual. No two journeys are the same, and as a result, no two people will have the same interactions, be spoken to the same way, or even be led along hallways by the same nurses and doctors. Subsequently, no one narrative of the space can ever be complete. No single characterization, not even Carroll's, is psychologically deep—the participant can only ever map his or her own navigations through space and time onto the characters' psyches. Add to this the alterations of space to include the fanciful imagery and characters of Carroll's fictions, and time and site themselves become malleable, interpretive, and reflexive. However, where Lehmann suggests that this type of theatre, the theatre of speed and surface, describes a passive set of impulses that waylays the imagination, I suggest that they call participants to do *more* within the bounds of site. Literature provides beginnings, middles, and ends, with textual signifiers that have broad, abstract, signifiers. Delimiting texts in spaces, however expansive, restricts the abstractions of language. Stripping away linearity and the ability to narrate the self in space further inhibits external opportunities for things to mean in concert with each other. In such circumstances individuals are forced to map individual meanings onto objects, persons, and the site itself. Rather than producing a narrative *read* by participants, *Then She Fell* forces them into a crisis in which participants have to interpret the speed and surface of the world they have been dropped into. As such, *immersive theatre* is post dramatic theatre, destabilizing the primacy of drama, and of literature. Lehmann continues:

In post-dramatic forms of *theatre*, staged text (*if* text is staged) is merely a component in a gestic, musical, visual, etc., total composition. The rift between the

---

[24] Lehmann, Hans-Thies, trans. Karen Jürs-Munby. Postdramatic Theatre (New York: Routledge, 2006), 16.

discourse of the text and that of the theatre can open up all the way to an openly exhibited discrepancy or even unrelatedness.[25]

Theatrical practice in the immersive theatre opens up such a discrepancy. However, productions such as *Then She Fell* call upon participants to cede control of interpretation in exchange for sensual, visceral, and manipulatable impulses. Seductive though they may be, these performances engage auditors as actors in strictly circumscribed sites and events masquerading as unique, individual, and intimate one-time experiences. The sites of the immersive theatre therefore become exemplars of the post dramatic—post-textual events that develop through a synthesis of communications, hypertexts, and experiences occurring inside and outside of theatrical space/time.

Housed in sites, images and signs provoke the participatory interchange that, in Lehmann's definition, becomes the "collective" foundation of theatre—as-event. In *Sleep No More*, participants become homogenous specters through the use of masks—until touched or spoken to by a performer. In *Then She Fell*, participants bond through acts of voyeurism and intimate tête-à-têtes with actors. *Queen of the Night* pushes strangers to break bread together while flirty company members touch and manipulate the crowd. These interactions, occurring as they do in physical or *real* theatre-space, secret away the complex of expectations, boundaries, and media informing the mores and behaviors of participants before they ever cross the site's threshold. In the immersive theatre, the experience of site exceeds the boundaries of collective experience. While this may also be true of other theatrical forms, in immersive formats the emphasis on pre-performance preparation occurs in the interest of controlling participant responses—media and imagery reinforce the boundaries of the kinetic, imaginary, worlds engaged by site.

Interwoven into both habitable and virtual spaces, immersive theatre therefore uses site for both aesthetic and commercial effect. The shifting nature of theatrical signs, in Lehmann's view, justifies the creation of the term *post dramatic*. Similarly, immersive theatres' utilization of signs in imagery and site responds to post dramatic impulses in technology and culture. As a critical example, *Queen of the Night* declines textual referents to focus on sensuality. Deemphasizing collectivity and narrative, the production prefers the "speed and surface" of spectacle. Effectively, I argue, this format conforms to the commercial, branded aspects of immersive forms—individuating participant experiences based on a neoliberal model of subjectivity and self-reliance.

Whereas the physical conditions of sites change radically between immersive productions (warehouses, schools, clubs, and etc.), the internal ideologies deployed in these spaces retain similar points of reference. Sites in the immersive theatre serve as conduits—either through the materials provided before entrée into the site-proper, or the physical site itself—into the otherworldly experience of the immersion. Josephine Machon, in her work *Immersive Theatres* (2013) underscores the fact that immersive sites are places "Where the audience-participant is imaginatively and sceno-graphically reoriented in another place, an otherworldly-world that requires

---

[25] Lehmann, Hans-Thies, trans. Karen Jürs-Munby. Postdramatic Theatre (New York: Routledge, 2006), 46.

navigation according to its own rules of logic."[26] In these terms, site's importance to immersive theatre lies significantly in its atmospheric qualities, but, Machon continues, "Whereas in games practice this occurs in a conceptual space, in immersive theatre a central feature of the experience is that this otherworldly-world is *both* a conceptual, imaginative space *and* an inhabited physical space." The conceptual and imaginary site of performance increasingly includes guidelines, controlling the imaginations and expectations of audiences.

As the "other-worldly world" in *Queen of the Night*, The Diamond Horseshoe provides a provenance associated with vintage luxury, facilitating the creation of imaginative and virtual expectations of the production for prospective participants. Lehmann's definition exposes the shift towards image and sense-experience, allowing for an expansion of the theatrical ground. If Lehmann helps situate what immersion *is* then Patrice Pavis's definition of site-specific performance illuminates what it is *not*:

This term [site-specific performance] refers to a staging and performance conceived on the basis of a place in the real world (ergo, outside of established theatre). A large part of the work has to do with researching a place, often an unusual one, that is imbued with history or permeated with atmosphere: an airplane hangar, unused factory, city neighborhood, house or apartment. The insertion of a classical or modern text in this 'found space' throws new light on it, give it an unsuspected power, and places the audience at an entirely different relationship to the text, the place and the purpose for being there.[27]

In Pavis's definition, the site of performance in the site-specific aesthetic provides a significant influence on the performance event. The historical apparatus latent in a place proves important to the methods and structures in site-specific work, provoking an artistic response that engages with the histories, socio-politics, and publics served by the site now and in the past. This level of social responsibility is rarely, if ever, true of immersive performances. Disused spaces, historically relevant spaces, or atmospheric spaces are utilized specifically to serve the marketplace.

Given *Queen of the Night's* ultimately narrow window of provocative impulses (sexual liberation or straight-laced inhibition), the production provides a surprisingly large spatial arrangement that traverses virtual, historical, and physical landscapes. For example, the Diamond Horsehoe's history as Billy Rose's nostalgia-driven nightclub provides a rare instance in which the production's impulse towards sensual consumption and atmospherics mirrors the original use of the site. Placing Pavis's definition beside Lehmann's, site-specific theatre implies a level of social engagement, whereas immersive theatre represents the "speed and surface" referenced by Lehmann. To borrow a phrase from a *Forbes* article on *Then She Fell*, this is theatre for "the videogame generation"—a specific mix of game theory, sensory overload, and mysterious occurrences designed to exploit site to suit the exigencies of consumers familiar with open-world videogames, interactive entertainments, and non-linear narratives.[28]

---

[26] Machon, Josephine. Immersive Theatres: Intimacy and Immediacy in Contemporary Performance (New York: Palgrave Macmillan, 2013), 63.

[27] Pavis, Patrice. "Site-Specific Performance" in Dictionary of the Theatre: Terms, Concepts, and Analysis (Toronto: University of Toronto Press 1998), 337–338.

[28] Porges, Seth. "Theater for the Videogame Generation," Forbes, October 29, 2012 [Online] Available: *http://www.forbes.com*/sites/sethporges/2012/10/29/theater-for-the-video-game-generation/.

Videogames, virtual reality, and other technological forms, have begun popping into the consumer landscape with regularity. Smartphones, smart watches, and a vast range of other wearable tech have created what is now referred to as "The Internet of Things" (IoT). Jacob Morgan defines this term in an article for Forbes:

> Simply put this is the concept of basically connecting any device with an on and off switch to the Internet (and/or to each other). This includes everything from cell phones, coffee makers, washing machines, headphones, lamps, wearable devices and almost anything else you can think of. This also applies to components of machines, for example a jet engine of an airplane or the drill of an oil rig. As I mentioned, if it has an on and off switch then chances are it can be a part of the IoT. The analyst firm Gartner says that by 2020 there will be over 26 billion connected devices…that's a lot of connections (some even estimate this number to be much higher, over 100 billion). The IoT is a giant network of connected "things" (which also includes people). The relationship will be between people-people, people-things, and things-things.[29]

Similar to the expansion of the virtual events produced for the pre-performance landscapes of immersive theatre, the IoT removes the boundaries of real time and space from the practice of communication—even automating parts of that communication according to pre-determined, but increasingly flexible, scripts. As self-contained sites, sites that depend on participant interaction to fulfill their own scripts, immersive spaces have become a metaphorical plane upon which this future is already occurring. Far beyond a website or e-mailed communication, entry into the immersive theatre means, not just inhabiting Machon's "otherworldly world," but navigating, interacting with, and defining that world on an individual basis. The vision of such spaces seems, as with the IoT itself, to be novel and expansive. With the interconnectedness of all things and people, all things and people come closer together—a utopic vision of space-time.

Henri Lefebvre, in his arguably prophetic book *The Production of Space* (1991), delivers an analysis of space eerily similar to contemporary technologies of site and creation long before any real discussion of an "Internet of Things" existed:

> It [space] embodies at best a technological utopia, a computer simulation of the future, or of the possible, within the framework of the real—the framework of the existing mode of production. The starting-point here is a knowledge which is at once integrated into, and integrative with respect to, the mode of production. The technological utopia in question is a common feature not just of many science fiction novels, but also of all kinds of projects concerned with space, be they those of architecture, urbanism, or social planning.[30]

The technological utopia, "a common feature of many science fiction novels," describes modes of production as integrated with knowledge, and vice versa. This

[29] Morgan, Jacob. "A Simple Explanation of 'The Internet of Things." Forbes, May 5, 2014. *http://www.forbes.com/sites/jacobmorgan/*2014/05/13/simple-explanation-internet-things-that-anyone-can-understand/.
[30] Lefebvre, Henri., trans. David Nicholson-Smith. The Production of Space (Malden, MA: Blackwell Publishing, 1991 orig. 1974), 9.

sounds much like Morgan's description of the IoT. Similar again to the immersive theatre, Lefebvre's analysis of spaces as "simulations of the possible within frameworks of the real" invokes any of the *immersive* production formats discussed so far. As self-contained and virtual worlds, immersive theatrical landscapes produce expansive spaces that realize closely monitored simulations of the possible. When combined with the sociopolitical ideology of the *neoliberal* consumer environment of the IoT, however, Lefebvre's vision quickly turns dystopic, less *Star Trek: The Next Generation*, and more *1984*.

This is not to say that *The Production of Space* is not critical of the ability to read space, in many ways anticipating the creation of the Internet of Things. Throughout the rest of his book, Lefebvre systematically reviews space and the relationships that compose and mold it. Interconnected, inclusive, and flexible, spaces are regarded as fluid, *readable*, containers.[31] Making a call for the considered analysis of spatial use, he also relates the difficulties endemic to doing so:

> It is no longer a matter of the space of this or the space of that: rather, it is in its totality or global aspect that needs not only to be subjected to analytic scrutiny (a procedure which is liable to furnish merely an infinite series of fragments and cross-sections subordinate to the analytic project), but also to be *engendered* by and within theoretical understanding [emphasis original].[32]

This process of spatial analysis can only be realized, according to Lefebvre, through time *and* space. Or as he describes, "The historical and its consequences, the 'diachronic,' the 'etymology' of locations in the sense of what happened at a particular spot or place and thereby changed it—all of this becomes inscribed in space."[33] With regard to, say, *Queen of the Night*, the legibility of space breaks down upon closer analysis. While the production presents a façade of unified space/time realized through the insistent messaging of renovation, installation, marketing, and bodies, examining the cultural history produced in that space fragments and dismantles its innuendoes. Space, therefore, represents a layering of effects and significations that respond to both internal contexts (those that relate to an individual's experience) and external ones (those that relate to the events taking, or that have taken, place in X space—real or imagined). Following Alison Landsberg's *Prosthetic Memory: The Transformation of American Remembrance in the Age of Mass Culture* (2004), these two contexts become fluid-readily shifting and reacting to places both virtual and material, to construct (or reconstruct) frames of history, memory, experience, and presence. As Landsberg writes, "*Prosthetic Memory* asks scholars and intellectuals to take seriously the popularity of new cultural surfaces, such as experiential museums, and demands their recognition of the power of these new media to affect people and shape their politics."[34] Simultaneously enmeshed in, and descriptive of, The Internet of Things, neoliberalism, and constructed history, the immersive theatre rehearses what happens when virtuality gains priority over the

---

[31] Lefebvre, 15.
[32] Lefebvre, 37.
[33] Lefebvre, 37.
[34] Landsberg, Alison. Prosthetic Memory: The Transformation of American Remembrance in the Age of Mass Culture (New York: Columbia University, 2004), 21.

corporality of real-time performance events and their spatial circumstances. Taking Lefebvre and Landsberg's viewpoints together, mediatized and material experiences no longer represent discernably different experiences of space.

Queen of the Night pays unusual attention to sensual interactions, over and above narrative impulses. Indeed, the preeminence of bodily experience in these spaces may represent the logical extension of current cultural trends, especially with relation to virtuality and technological evolution. Robin Nelson, in *Mapping Intermediality in Performance* (2010) expands on this tectonic movement:

> Contemporary theatre practice may well be less concerned with offering meanings than pleasures and experiences, the frisson of momentary dislocation of normative bearings and the opening up of new perceptual modes extending the range of human experience; and perhaps even projecting us into the post human.[35]

The "momentary dislocation of normative bearings" sums up, not just the use of space in the immersive theatre, but a benchmark for defining *immersion* as a conceptual tool—a tool used for something other than marketing. Dislocation, however, comes in a multitude of forms. In *Queen of the Night*, this takes the form of a burlesque nightclub, while in *Sleep No More* or *Then She Fell*; the scenic efforts replicate places that seem familiar: an asylum, a bar, a candy shop, or a bedroom. In these latter instances, the familiarity of constructed sites determine a protocol for their exploration, as well as a frame in which they can become *other* through telltale signs. For example, In *Sleep No More* a bathtub holds an eel, and in *Then She Fell* the floor of the asylum falls away to reveal a pond—each signaling that the seeming familiarity of spaces is at odds with their corporal reality. *Queen of the Night* forecloses the strangeness elicited in these latter productions in exchange for a framing of site delimited by homogeneity—what you see is what you get. For while Billy Rose's haunted ballroom informs the excess and spectacle of *Queen of the Night*, the new Horseshoe flattens the site's historical context into an undifferentiated, capital-driven experience; one that replaces the altered realities of other events with a monolithic focus on sensuality and nostalgia.

Nostalgia and commercialism often cohabit in the theatre. However, unlike conventional theatrical events that take place, say, framed by a proscenium arch, so-called immersive events such as *The Queen of the Night* create problems of definition and genera. Site-specific theatre, interactive theatre, participatory theatre, promenade theatre, environmental theatre—all appear to fall somewhere under the aegis of *immersion*, with most identifying the specificity of site as a core convention of the theatrical event. Yet *immersion* implies more than these terms suggest. Especially with regard to space, the expectation of the participant being surrounded, engulfed, or otherwise overwhelmed, infuses the concept of *immersion*—transforming site into an interactive actor-participant with its own agenda and agency. As Josephine Machon describes in *Immersive Theatres*, "Immersive theatre actively demonstrates how space is the palpable medium where the historical memory of simultaneous activity is a

---

[35] Nelson, Robin, Sarah Bay-Cheng, Chiel Kattenbelt, and Andy Lavender eds. Mapping Intermediality in Performance (Amsterdam: Amsterdam University Press, 2010), 20.

constant *praesance*."[36] In this, space serves a paradoxical role. On one hand *praesance*, or being in-the-moment, dictates experience as the crowning achievement of immersion. Yet space constructs the experience of the participant—it is palpable and navigable, containing memory and activity. Space becomes the means of conveyance into another world, as well as the world itself. With regard to many exemplars of immersion, the in-betweenness of such theatrical spaces often expands the potential for audience engagement, calling seductively for participants to imbue objects and sites with new and varied meanings in the interest of narrating their own experience.

Ascribing agency to the sites of immersive theatre proves crucial to discerning the difference, or nuance, provided by the term *immersive* itself. Concretely, site-as-actor often serves as the primary contact point between production and participant in immersive environments. Finding themselves freed from the typical restraints incumbent upon audiences, participants wander through transformed sites installed with artistic flourishes, sometimes totally alone. Spaces become an enigmatic forest of signs and signifiers, with participants distributing and mapping meanings across as much of the site as can be explored. These experiences have proved seductive, inciting large online communities to map both immersive spaces and prospective experiences to be had with performers.[37] Overall, the immersive phenomenon takes on many aspects of a game or puzzle, especially of the kind created by current technologies—interactive worlds engaged in the first-person and constructed to appear real. As the ability to create virtual worlds becomes increasingly attainable through such technologies as VR goggles, smart-phone applications, or Google Glass, immersive theatre also focuses similarly on an experience of virtuality—creating an inclusive interface for participants known as *intermedial* performance. In *Mapping Intermediality in Performance*, Robin Nelson and Chiel Kattenbelt describe this term's special significance to theatre, asserting that

Theatre is distinctive, among the arts and media, in its capacity to stage other media in a process of theatricalization, which incorporates them under the conditions of their established media specificity without transforming them (as in transmediality), and without abandoning its own specificity of liveness in the here and now.[38]

While Robin Nelson goes on to suggest that this view of liveness may be troubled by such things as virtual performances, they nonetheless established performance as a process-based phenomenon where space maintains interrelationships with other media, but remains a fixed point of reference. Paradigmatically, this terminology allows *immersion* and *immersive* space to exist without muddying the waters searching for a single, elusive definition.

In its attention to individual, sensual experience, *Queen of The Night* places a high priority on being in-the-moment. However, it remakes the Diamond Horseshoe

---

[36] Emphasis original. Machon defines praesence via Deleuze on pg. 109, expanding on the concept in later discussions: "This is an 'absolute' experience of being 'in the moment,' a constant praesance, ascribes the full force of the experience to the moment of being in the event itself..." Machon, Josephine. Immersive Theatres: Intimacy and Immediacy in Contemporary Performance (New York: Palgrave Macmillan, 2013), 143.

[37] A partial list of such sites and communities may be found in my bibliography. However, it must be noted that such communities appear and disappear as certain events come and go.

[38] Nelson, Robin and Chiel Kattenbelt, Andy Lavender, and Sarah-Bay Cheng, eds. Mapping Intermediality in Performance (Amsterdam: Amsterdam University Press, 2010), 19.

into a commercial medium where receiving personalized performances depends on individual luck and ingenuity as opposed to choice. Entering the space comes at a high price (higher than good seats at most Broadway productions), and with a tiered pricing system that includes varying levels of interaction, food, and drink. The production's website and ticketing provide a glimpse at the wide, and highly unequal, range of experiences available:

> QUEEN OF THE NIGHT is a decadent fusion of theater, cuisine, circus, and nightlife that welcomes guests into a wholly interactive entertainment experience. All of The Queen's guests will receive a welcome cocktail, passed canapés, and full sit-down dinner complete with decanters of wine. Dress to please the Queen. Cocktail or gala attire required. The Queen will deny access to guests who are not appropriately dressed.

ULTIMATE RESERVATION

The Ultimate Reservation promises esteemed guests our highest level of service and access. In addition to everything included in the Premium Reservation, you're invited behind the scenes to indulge in a selection of delicacies personally chosen by our Executive Chef, and assisted with your choice of a premium wine to accompany your dinner. You will then be escorted to your VIP reserved seats for personalized table service throughout the rest of your evening.

PREMIUM RESERVATION

The Premium Reservation grants you admission to the Diamond Horseshoe and all of the Queen's festivities including cocktails, passed canapés, and full sit-down dinner complete with decanters of wine. Premium guests will be welcomed with VIP reserved preferred seats and private cocktail service at the table. You will also receive a gift from the Queen which entitles you to free-flowing drinks from our Mad Distillery Bar.

GALA RESERVATION

The Gala Reservation grants you admission to the Diamond Horseshoe and all of the Queen's planned festivities. You will receive a welcome cocktail from our Mad Distillery Bar, passed canapés and a sit-down dinner complete with decanters of wine. Cash bar is available for additional beverage purchases. PLEASE NOTE: Gala Reservations are general admission seating; there are no assigned seats.

QUEEN'S CHOICE

Queen's Choice is a highly customized, exclusive QUEEN OF THE NIGHT experience that is personally tailored to each guest by our VIP concierge team. Reservations can be made at concierge@queenofthenightnyc.com.[39]

The cost for these tiers comes to $140 (Gala), $190 (Premium) and $390 (Ultimate). The "Queen's Choice" package includes no prices, but it might be assumed to include an even higher cost (above and beyond the "Ultimate" experience). The installation of this hierarchy, from the moment participants purchase tickets, immediately recalls attention to the neoliberal aspects of immersive production in this, and other performances. In my own experiences with immersive theatre in New York City, I have never encountered such a clearly defined pricing scale associated with the potential intimacy and services of the production. *Sleep No More* relies mostly on luck to attain the most intimate "one-on-one" experiences, and *Then She Fell* leads participants on pre-determined performance tracks that are not correlated with ticket pricing. *Queen of the Night* establishes the class-hierarchy of the event and our role inside the space, from the very moment of purchase.

Reviewing the production for *The New York Times*, Charles Isherwood describes some of his experiences with the space and its denizens:

> Although there is a sprig of drama involved-characters modeled on the principals in Mozart's "Magic Flute" have central roles in the floor show— the foursquare aim of this meticulously produced spectacle is to satiate appetites other than traditionally dramatic ones. Just how sated you will be depends on chance, to a degree. As with 'Sleep No More,' every individual's experience will be different. You might drink, dine and watch the performance, most of which takes place on a raised platform in the middle of the ballroom-size dining room, without being accosted by any of the "butlers," as the wranglers who spirit customers away for private encounters are called. Or you could be lassoed (literally) almost the moment you descend the marble staircase leading to the festivities, as my companion was, and led off into a private chamber for some intimate talk about intimate matters. ("Have you ever been in love?") Or you could find yourself, as I did, shoeless and sitting in a fur-and-mirror-lined boudoir with a pert young woman making goo-goo eyes at you as she strokes your face with a feather.[40]

The ballroom, boudoir, chamber, and staircase provide the venues for intimate, flirtatious encounters with the butlers, but these often occur by "chance." Titillation, and the fantasy of encounters with the scantily clad actors, reproduces a version of desires encouraged by floor shows starring Billy Rose's 6'2" chorus girls in the 194's. Taken abruptly through the wrought-iron boundary of the ballroom's center, a female butler danced seductively on a platform in front of me (I peeked). She stroked and

---

[39] Queen of The Night: http://queenofthenightnyc.com/.
[40] Isherwood, Charles. "A Circus of Intimate Sensation: Twisting, Touching and Teasing in 'Queen of the Night,'" The New York Times, February 2, 2014.

touched my face and back. However, unlike Isherwood's private one-on-one, this was done in full-view of other participants. At once voyeuristic and intimate, encounters with the performers present themselves comparably to those promoted by Punchdrunk's *Sleep No More*, but without the narrative pretension extending from either Shakespeare or Alfred Hitchcock. The sexuality on display in *Queen of the Night*, while still of the PG variety, maintains itself with the discipline of the strip-club: look but don't touch, indulge, but not too much. However, notwithstanding the difficulty of attaining these semi-accessible encounters, the site itself structures the hierarchical relationship of participants to spaces and bodies through a resurrection of its original use. Spatial logic, in *The Queen of the Night*, offers our imaginations the fleeting feeling of being desired and desiring, of being pampered and important-but with a constant reminder of the one-night-only ephemerality of it all, and all in the spirit of capitalistic competition that made Rose a lasting businessman.

Reading the Diamond Horseshoe's situation underscores that ephemerality, joining the faded aesthetic of the original structure with the outlandish conceptions of Randy Weiner, and his co-producer Simon Hammerstein. To achieve these effects, the Horseshoe's renovation required homages to the chorus-girl spectacles of the late 1930s and '40s art-deco design, and the preservation of historic details. To bring the spectacle up-to-date, the production also uses elements of post-modern burlesque and variety performance, with architectural renovations to match the cabaret-like costuming of the butlers. Maintaining portions of Rose's original design proves critical to this strategy, encouraging participants to view the ballroom as a historical conduit-a world in which normative inhibitions seem passé.

Using Machon's terms, *Queen of The Night* takes Billy Rose's historical context as its conceptual space, but remodels the inhabited physical space with the gaudy trappings of 2006's pre-crash excesses. *Vanity Fair* affirms that, "Beneath the neon, the space is configured just as it was in Rose's day. An extensive renovation left the staircase paint peeling."[41] That staircase conveys both a literal and figurative descent. The peeling paint, unkempt stacks of champagne flutes, and elegant deco curves of the stairwell, all suggest our tardiness to the party: one that began long before our entry, and may continue long after we leave. As the Horseshoe's literal threshold, the three flights spark tension, anticipation, and curiosity. Like Disney princesses and princes, we make our way down to a climactic and sumptuous party-a celebrity ball where our celebrity is a fiction.

In this case, resurrecting the Diamond Horseshoe reflects, not a reengagement with Broadway's golden age, but a post-capitalist paean for the golden age of millennial profiteering. *W* magazine, producing a similar article as *Vanity Fair* about the $20 million dollar renovation of the Diamond Horseshoe, describes the triumphant excess of the space's makeover:

"The space is like a cross between a church, an opera house, and a bordello," added Giovanna Battaglia, the creative director of the project and a *W* contributing fashion editor. In conjunction with Douglas Little, who has designed window displays for Bergdorf Goodman, Battaglia transformed the dilapidated location into a gilded

---

[41] Monahan, Patrick, "The Diamond Horseshoe, the World War II-Era Nightclub Resurrected by Randy Weiner and Simon Hammerstein," Vanity Fair. January 24, 2014. Accessed August 2, 2014, http://www.vanityfair.com/online/daily/2014/01/diamond-horseshoe-nightclub-simon-hammerstein.

lily of surrealism, with hammered-gold floors, green velvet stage curtains held back by four-foot-long hands, and a bejeweled ceiling inspired by Catholic monstrances. She enlisted the designer Thom Browne to dream up fetishistic costumes like butler suits accessorized with phalluses.[42]

This church/opera house/bordello, full of fetishistic costumes, constructs a fantasy of exclusivity, of being desired guests at an event most have paid a great deal to attend.

Queen of the Night, with its weird, cognitive dissonance of sex and restraint, to some degree fits the bill of site-specific theatre as described by Pavis. After all, where else but the Diamond Horseshoe could such *constructed history* be interpolated so effortlessly with the reality of spatial use? However, to conflate *Queen of the Night's* use of space with site-specific theatre is to elide the specificity of site in social, political, contexts. Beyond the apparently neoliberal aspects of the performance, the celebratory conjuring up of pre-recession wealth, and the hierarchical arrangement of audiences, the space merely cites itself as a reason for the gathering without critically commenting on the undercurrent of classist, capitalistic, dogma pinned to its former use. In terms of site-specific performance this production illustrates, conversely, how the conjoining of prosthetic memory with spatial analysis creates socially engaged site-use. It is difficult, for example, not to read Mike Pearson's description of his project in *Site-Specific Performance* (2010) without reflecting on parallels with Lefebvre:

I suggest that the conventions and techniques of the auditorium may be inappropriate or inadequate to addressing "site." And that site-specific performance is other than a transposition and modification of stage practices. If the stage is essentially *synecdochic*—in the which limited resources stand in for a complete picture, as when a table and chairs suggests a domestic scene-site is frequently a site of plenitude, its inherent characteristics, manifold effects, and unruly elements always liable to leak, spill and diffuse into performance: "site-specific work has to deal with, embrace, and cohabit with existing factors of scale, architecture, chance, accident, incident."[43]

Allowing the book's project to remain unencumbered by theoretically pigeonholing site-specific performance, Pearson sets out instead to create a work for practical application. Through an informal series of guideposts, he aims to "encourage further initiatives in performance."[44] Like Lefebvre and Landsberg, who aim to create a theoretical structure for space, time, and cultural memory, Pearson's opening lines evoke the fluidity of performance with relation to space, time, place, and individual experience. For immersive theatrical events, that fluidity accompanies overwhelming sensual data available during a given performance, rendering a complex realignment of space and time with regard to asynchronous, decentered experiences.

Mike Pearson, whose work has more often been characterized as site-specific, began using immersive tropes before the term formally existed as a description for theatre. As such, Pearson's work with Welsh company Brith Gof provides data concerning the use of immersive tactics and aesthetics, but ones that consciously

---

[42] Lawrence, Vanessa. "The Diamond Horseshoe,,"W Magazine, January 17, 2014. http://www.wmagazine.com/culture/2014/01/diamond-horseshoe-nyc-nightclub/photos/.

[43] Pearson, Mike. Site-Specific Performance (London: Palgrave Macmillan, 2010), 1.

[44] Pearson, 2.

avoid neoliberal models and the label 'immersive'. *Goddodin* (1998), based on an ancient Welsh epic, took place in a site that engulfed participants in the intensity of battle. The company's use of space illustrates aesthetic immersion-a retroactive defining of the performance that alludes to similar methods of sensual engagement as, say *Queen of the Night* or *Sleep No More*, but that retain the integrity of social and historical contexts in its use of space-a historical engagement that proves less *virtual* in its engagement than parallel to present political struggles. In the company's words:

> The impetus to create the performance came with the darkest days of "Thatcherism," a time when Margaret Thatcher herself proclaimed society dead. Of course, the metaphorical implications of the poem were self-evident. But in deciding to create a large-scale work, at the limits of our ability to achieve it both technically and physically, we aimed to echo the folly of the Gododdin, the small struggling with the impossibly greater. We wanted to constitute political theatre as sophistication and complexity, elaborating dramatic material and detail in all available media simultaneously, to work with the friction between the sensibilities and procedures of theatre and rock music and with anachronism.
>
> *Gododdin* was conceived, constructed, and initially presented for three nights late in December 1998, in the engine-shop of the enormous, disused Rover car factory in Cardiff, itself a potent symbol of economic decline and industrial decay.[45]

Goddodin not only reached backwards to revive a key document of Welsh culture, but reached forward in time and space to critically engage with "Thatcherism" and the destruction of livelihoods through the dismantling of Welsh industry. And, in the midst of this highly physical performance, participants found themselves in the midst of a struggle—between the old battle and the new social struggle, between Welsh and English languages, and "the small struggling with the impossibly greater." As described in *The Independent's* review, participants had to pay close attention to their surroundings, or risk being a casualty of the battle themselves:

> The performance begins almost imperceptibly, as Lis Hughes Jones recites from a central position on the balcony. Then, to guttural blasts from the taped soundtrack, the doors open. As the traffic speeds by in the street outside, Test Department enters on a fantastical cart made of wood and scrap metal, torchlit. In the male players' costumes of maroon kilts, black cloaks, and Dr. Martens, they circle the hall and climb to the percussion instruments wailing on the gantry. Then come the players; four men and two women. After ritual grooming and heroic postures, their haughty demeanor turns to aggressive sham. Oil drums collide in midair and the audience realises that quick

---

[45] "Brith Gof: Goddodin" [Online] Accessed: 7 February 2015,.
http://humanitieslab.stanford.edu/brithgof/19.

reflexes are needed to avoid the tyres whirled on ropes. The cars take a fearful beating.[46]

This description highlights the futility and frustration of the epic's violence. The David and Goliath story of industry/colonialism vs. livelihoods/nationalism ends with the defeat of the Welsh people—a defeat to which participants bear witness, and are indeed a part of whether they like it or not. _The Scotsman_ concurred:

> Promenade Theatre is too wan a description for this spectacle, since the audience is dragged willy-nilly into the action, and will have to keep attentive to avoid the performers, who leap in their midst, swing massive rubber tyres in their direction or hurl steel barrels either into pools of water or at the pillars behind which the prescient spectator will cower.[47]

The reviews never mention the term _immersive_, yet the installation of a massive space with scenery and props, the participation of audiences, the reconstitution of site, and the sensual force of the performance, all point towards contemporary immersive aesthetics. Even so, the inescapable difference between _Goddodin_ and _The Queen of the Night_, or any of the range of New York performances that self-describe as immersive, are highlighted by the description and reviews of _Goddodin_. Drawing again from the notion of _constructed history_ and pre-performance expectations, the viscerality of _Goddodin_ is real: avoiding the flailing warriors, with their tires and car-hood shields, becomes a necessity. _Queen of the Night_ evokes viscerality through lustful depictions, through flirtation, and through the appropriation of site, but these all prove illusory in the real-time context of the production. In terms of sociopolitical context, _Goddodin_ features a concise and powerful critical awareness, whereas _Queen of the Night_ revels in, and reproduces, the excesses of pre-recession America without critical attention to, or acknowledgement of, present social, historical, or political forces.

Mike Pearson defines the artistic and dramaturgical activities that create productions like _Goddodin_ in _Site-Specific Performance_, providing clues as to the usefulness of the company's practices near to the birth of immersive theatre as a term of art. If _Goddodin_ might be redefined as _immersive_ (in addition to site-specific), then the collection of site-practices engaged by Brith Gof may represent an approachable, flexible means of defining socially engaged _immersive_ practices. The potential to fuse aesthetic and experiential notions with branding practices could shift the potential use-value of sites in New York City and beyond. Mike Pearson writes,

But in addressing the very particularities of its engagement with a location, any choreographic account of site-specific performance as a thing will necessitate detailed description, paying equal attention to that which is of the site and that which is brought to the site, the inextricable binding of place and artwork, to demonstrate its uniqueness.

---

[46] "Brith Gof: Goddodin" [Online] Accessed: 7 February 2015. http://humanitieslab.stanford.edu/brithgof/19.
[47] "Brith Gof: Goddodin" [Online] Accessed: 7 February 2015. http://humanitieslab.stanford.edu/brithgof/19.

This might resemble what Michael Shanks and I called a *deep map* (Pearson and Shanks, 64–66): "an attempt to record and represent the substance, grain, and patina of a particular place, through juxtapositions and interweavings of the historical and the contemporary, the political and the poetic, the factual and the fictional, the academic and the aesthetic…depth not as profundity but as topographic and cultural density." In this it is perhaps akin to anthropologist Clifford Geertz's *thick description*: the detailed and contextual description of cultural phenomena, to discern the complexities behind the action, and from which the observer is not removed (Geertz) It may further reference his *blurred genre*: as Shanks and I appropriated it, "a mixture of narration and scientific practices, an integrated, interdisciplinary, intertextual and creative approach to recording, writing, and illustrating the material past" (Pearson and Shanks, 131).[48]

The *deep map*, if applied to so-called *immersive* forms, defines the holistic confluence of a site with aesthetics, history, and virtuality. The stakes of applying this set of practices becomes most evident near the end of the quotation, where Pearson describes "writing, and illustrating the material past." In other words, the structuration of the past in space represents an affective act of recording and imagining history. Thus, in *Queen of the Night*, when the record concludes that the past begins and ends in the virtual, in expectation, and in unsatisfied desires, it elides the dramaturgy of space and time in favor of sensuality and image-returning to Lehmann, *Queen of the Night* represents the "speed and surface" of performance without the *deep map* or the *thick description* that socially enlivens performance events like *Goddodin*.

If the holistic site, in Pearson's view, interweaves the spatial and aesthetic with the past, present, and even future, then the constructed history of sites like The Diamond Horseshoe, the asylum of *Then She Fell* or the McKittrick Hotel of *Sleep No More* all depend on an implicit text. Even if that text is fully devised, narrative still pervades and authorizes immersive theatre-spaces. For *Queen of the Night*, the floor show includes a love story of sorts; *Sleep No More* depends on *Macbeth*; and *Then She Fell* on both *Alice in Wonderland* and *Through the Looking Glass*. In the spirit of expanding the theatrical ground—one that includes virtual spaces and messages as well as real, sensual experiences—texts become embedded in immersive theatrical sites. As such, the supposed lack of texts in immersive experiences often, ironically, indicates their expansive presence. The space of immersive performance absorbs texts and diffuses them across carefully composed images, experiences, and performances. Andrew Sofer, in his book *Dark Matter* (2013) expresses such a model in reference to Punchdrunk Theatre Company's *Sleep No More*. Sofer's description of this space is worth quoting at length:

> Aside from invisible props like Macbeth's dagger and offstage figures like Godot, spectral reading illuminates the impact of phantom presences whose substance is not, in the first instance, rhetorical…Thus *Sleep No More*, Punchdrunk Theatre's site-specific, phantasmagorical remix of *Macbeth* as filtered through Hitchcock and *The Shining*, is both nonmimetic and nonverbal. Far from synecdochically representing an elsewhere, the cavernous performance space is the total space of action. The "Manderley"

[48] Pearson, Mike. Site-Specific Performance (London: Palgrave Macmillan, 2010), 32.

bar remains a working bar with the audience can order a drink (even if it is cunningly ghosted by a double or doubles embedded elsewhere—a Platonic joke).[49]

Spectral reading as Sofer defines it "is a deliberate pun. Not only are we looking for ghosts we can see right through, invisible presences that cast no light themselves. We are expanding our investigative spectrum beyond material bodies and objects in order to discern hidden wavelengths beyond the reach of the naked (critical) eye."[50] In the case of Punchdrunk's work, as well as other immersive performances, text effectively becomes spatial. The process by which space exceeds synecdoche and morphs into place, enacting "nonmimetic" and "nonverbal" gestures that nonetheless conjure narrative forces, presents a critical flashpoint for the framing of contemporary performance. This is not to say that immersive work represents a novel expression of theatrical conventions, but rather that its spaces become places—imbued with memory, emotion, and sensuality—in ways that simultaneously refine, reflect, and reject cultural technologies ("surfaces"). In line with the interdisciplinary aspects described by Lefebvre, Landsberg, and Pearson, the novelty of immersive spaces lies in their coalescence—the refractions and interactions of forces inhuman and human, concrete and abstract, straightforward and labyrinthine. As evidenced in both *Queen of the Night* and *Goddodin*, the valences these texts produce differ broadly in practice. However, the textual/spatial/virtual all play a critical role in the structure and deployment of immersive sites.

Constructed history, as I have termed it here, is in many ways akin to spectral history. Behind, or beyond, the "total space of action" in the immersive theatre lays a void unfilled by cultural production. Mapped onto sites, these histories resonate with the technological revolution of the "Internet of Things," of videogames and virtual avatars, and of the curation of undefinable spatial identities. Given the way these theatres map onto space, linking virtual histories and personas onto concrete objects and events, I suggest that the commercial iterations of immersive theatre engage in a parasitic role with relation to site. The implications of the term *parasitic* generally provoke a negative response, but in this case its use relates only to the role site plays in relation to a performance event. The OED provides a primary usage of the term "parasite" as "an organism that lives on, in, or with an organism of another species, obtaining food, shelter, or other benefit; (now) *spec.* one that obtains nutrients at the expense of the host organism, which it may directly or indirectly harm." As opposed to *symbiosis*, where site and bodily performances might function cumulatively to create productions (e.g. *Goddodin)*, immersive sites present an opportunity for other theatrical aesthetics to exist through its intrinsic and extrinsic use-value. Whether through economic or aesthetic necessity, this parasitism proves reductive, distilling the depth of social and public space into surface forms and images ("speed and surface" again). *Sleep No More* was first transplanted from London to a disused school in Brookline, MA (2009), and then to a warehouse in Chelsea, (2012). *Then She Fell* (2013, 2014) takes place in a former parochial school in Brooklyn. *Queen of*

---

[49] Sofer, Andrew. Dark Matter: Invisibility in Drama, Theater, and Performance (Ann Arbor: university of Michigan Press, 2013), 9.

[50] Sofer, 5.

the Night, of course, takes place in the Diamond Horseshoe—ironically the only site of the three to make reference to the site's original cultural or public use. Where the production shuns textuality in favor of spectacle, that spectacle requires Billy Rose's ghost for its aesthetic and commercial foundation.

Beginning this discussion, I noted the definitional and generic confusion of labeling *immersive* theatre in relation to other associated theatrical forms. In doing so, I quoted Josephine Machon, and her criterion for such events in relation to the "otherworldly world" of the immersive theatre. In a subheading entitled "Total Immersion," Machon writes that, "Where total immersion occurs, there is always the experience of formalistic transformation in that the audience—participant is able to fashion her own 'narrative' and journey." This statement has born considerable scrutiny in the duration of this chapter, with site and site-use coming under fire for formalistic transformations that eliminate, or simply neglect, the social, political, and public in exchange for the sensual and experiential. Troublingly, the novelty of such experiences often trumps the critical examination of their inception and direction. With immersive, space itself appears to tumble into a rabbit-hole that disengages from the transformation of the social environment of New York City, but has the potential to explore the anxious interplay of technology and site, time and space, real and virtual.

CHAPTER 3

The Mists

Liz Ivkovich and Alysia Ramos

When it opened in October 2015, *The Mists* was a three-hour immersive dance theatre show. Featuring Morgaine Le Fey, Guinevere, the Lady of the Lake, Arthur, Lancelot, the King Stag, and the Queen of the Fey, *The Mists* had seven overlapping storylines. An eclectic ensemble of priestesses, fairies, stags, nuns, musicians, and a court supported the main characters. The production was fully integrated into Red Butte Garden's *Garden After Dark* event and was seen by an audience of nearly 7000 Salt Lake City residents.

(Liz) It is opening night. All 60(ish) of our performers are in place. The Garden twists, paths weaving trees and flower beds, steep and flat by turns, bending just out of sight. I am walking up a long hill, barely lit by the rope lights attached to the railing under my right hand. A booming "Night falls!" floats to me over the noise of the crowds. The battle between Arthur and the anthropomorphic stag beasts is starting, Merlin narrating the action in his deep bass. I consider rerouting my trajectory to catch the battle but continue up the hill instead. I stumble into a small family party; several kids and parents—all dressed as skiers. "This is my favorite part!," the daughter shouts. Pulling her mother's hand, she runs ahead. Lancelot stumbles out of a wayside into our path. Following him, Guinevere. Catching his shirt with her hand, she pulls him back in. Lancelot makes eye contact with the mother of this family party and flashes a cheeky grin. They are drawn into the wayside where Lance and Gwen arrange and rearrange furniture, flirtatiously molding their arms together. Laughing, they continue to play house until Lance takes a serious turn. Bending on one knee he looks up longingly at Gwen, she reaches as if to take his hand. On second thought—she slaps it away. Running ahead, she disappears up the path. We follow behind.

The invitation of *The Mists* was to come and experience something; stop and stay for a while, to let time stand still—to get lost. Getting lost is not the same as not knowing where you are, explains Rebecca Solnit in her book on the subject, *A Field Guide to Getting Lost*. It is instead a consciously chosen state of "voluptuous surrender" and an experience of being fully present within uncertainty and mystery (Solnit 6) To get lost in a work of art is to enter a space of possibility and transformation. *The Mists* was such a space; an epic tale with multiple points of departure and exit, a wild place beyond the theatre, and an extended hand to the audience to join us into this journey into the unknown, redefining the theatrical experience as one of active and intimate engagement between performer, landscape and audience.

(Alysia) It is spring 2014. I have just finished graduate school in modern dance at the University of Utah, and am breathing a sigh of relief that leaves me with the weight and force of the ocean receding at the change of tides. Liz still has two years to go, but is already struggling with the weight of the rising water. My son (six) and Liz's daughter (three) are keeping one another entertained arranging and rearranging chairs on the grassy lawn of the cafe as part of some elaborate game that has just been invented, while Liz and I occasionally look on and sip lattes. "When was the last time *we* were so enraptured in our work," we wondered aloud to one another? Our graduate school experience flashed across our memories—countless images of studios, theaters, studio theaters, sitting in darkened audiences, standing beneath blinding lights—awaiting magic, not finding it, empty seats, obligatory applause, genuine applause, congratulatory praise, ruthless critique, missing something, trying to find it. Starting over in the same way—studios, theaters, studio theaters. The goal was to find something—a voice, a style, a novel concept, a new idea, but it felt like a child constructing a sand castle too close to the water's edge, watching it continuously washed away, but carrying on just the same—with the sand and the shells and the water and the hope that this time it will be finished before the wave comes. Why not go somewhere new? Why not get lost?

Getting lost is a difficult proposition in Salt Lake City. The city is rich in ostensibly modern dance. Salt Lake City had once been at the forefront of the field. Repertory Dance Theater was the first full time modern dance company established outside of New York City by a grant from the Rockefeller Foundation in 1966. Another modern repertory company, Ririe-Woodbury Dance Company, began in 1964 at the University of Utah and shifted into full-time status with a grant from the Utah Arts Council in 1970. Additionally, there is a nationally recognized Children's Dance Theatre Company founded by Virginia Tanner that has been in existence since 1949. Utah's dance culture and community, like so many others, benefited greatly from the growth of national and local funding for the arts that occurred between the late 60s and early 80s. But unlike many other companies that were established during that time, Utah's early pioneering modern dance companies *still* exist (Habel 7–15).

All these companies have regular seasons on the proscenium stage with a large repertoire of classic works. Salt Lake is a place you can still see works by Isadora Duncan and Alwin Nikolais performed live, a treat for someone studying dance history, but offering very little that feels fresh. Even the newer commissions by current choreographers somehow come off feeling like relics of a modernism gone by; attractive if not entirely uniform, bodies performing a range of movements that include vocabulary from ballet and Doug Varone, gestures, no narrative, perhaps some humor, a lot of blank stares, a heavy dose of "fierceness," the arrangement of bodies against a white scrim. Yet, this is what modern dance is in Utah. It was birthed and nourished here and there is an audience cultivated by the decade long investment in what's become, in other cities, traditional modern. And while there's something intriguing about this living history, something lovely and nostalgic we could appreciate as dancers who came into the profession in the late nineties, we must admit we were bored by dance in Salt Lake.

The question became—what if we made the work we longed to see? It seems like an obvious question but not one we often asked ourselves. Mostly we thought about what we wanted to "say" or "do" with our dances, not what we wanted to experience. We reflected on works we'd seen in which we found ourselves utterly rapt; Punchdrunk's *Sleep No More*—an immersive theatre production, Christopher Williams's *Wolf-in-Skins*—a narrative dance opera, and Ellen Bromberg's site specific, abstract *Glyph* at the Utah Natural History Museum. These works framed their spaces and narratives, conversed with them, dusted off ideas and offered them up fresh and vital. These were works in which one could lose themselves as deeply as our children lost themselves in play. Three aspects burbled to the top as markers of the work we intended to make; immersive theatre, narrative, and ecological dance. Our path forward was unknown but our terrain became clear.

GARDEN AFTER DARK; STUMBLING INTO A STORY AND A SPACE

(Liz) I find myself, finally, at the Marriage to the Land. Morgaine Le Fey and Arthur sit on opposite sides of the large tree, framed by a circle of cement planters. This is the pivotal scene from *The Mists of Avalon,* Marion Zimmer Bradley's feminist retelling of Arthurian legend that inspired our script. From here begins the spiral of events that will lead to Arthur's betrayal of his half-sister Morgaine, and Avalon, her mystical home. But for now—they are in love. Arthur and Morgaine slowly circle the tree, drawn relentlessly towards each other, unaware of impending tragedy. A sudden onslaught of strollers explode through the space, lines of people loaded down by bags, coats and glow sticks, jarring me out of my reverie. The Lady of Lake and her Greek chorus of priestesses continue their single note hum, eyes focused on the scene. The swarm of people fades. A few of us are left in the scene—maybe twenty-five or thirty. A stillness settles, entranced. When the scene ends, the audience exhales—then claps. Though there are over one thousand people at *Garden After Dark* this evening, there were just the few of us here at that exact moment. Some who have begun to follow a favorite character through the story and some who have stumbled unexpectedly upon this scene. Hundreds of others roam the garden, some witnessing similar moments of our tale, many carrying on obliviously.

The Mists is a new addition to *Garden After Dark*, a well-established event that normally features the garden illuminated with decorative lighting, the paths dotted with craft stations, the occasional entertainer and an entryway hosting food trucks and vendors. When we approached Red Butte Garden about creating in their space, they asked us to partner with them on this event—a dream come true. Because of this ambitious and unprecedented partnership, *The Mists* reached a multigenerational audience of viewers who might not ordinarily see dance.

Like other cities, Salt Lake faces dwindling audiences for proscenium dance, aging patrons and supporters, decreases in government and foundation support and increased competition for viewership. Local solutions to these challenges fixate on "audience development" through better marketing or more education for existing programming. There are few conversations that imagine a radical restructuring of the existing models. What if the old dance formats just aren't working anymore? Could new programming attract new audiences?

Our built—in patrons at *Garden After Dark* ostensibly solved the audience question for us. The event gave us bodies but did not, however, assure us their attention, transforming a problem of attendance to a problem of engagement. Could we convince a group of unsuspecting theatregoers to get lost with us? The answer was a resounding yes and no. Our personal observations, a post event survey put out by Red Butte Garden and focus groups taken of staff, and cast reveal a complex picture. *The Mists* is alternately received as a delightful surprise, a secret discovery, an irritating disruption or a curious oddity by the unexpecting [sic] audience.

As dance-makers, we were used to sending dance into the front of house void. In the past, we'd heard criticisms, questions, compliments, but nothing like the raw reactions provoked by *The Mists*. From the delight of a child viewing a dancer close up for the first time, to a mother hurrying her family away from the "satanic rituals" of our priestess performers, we were shocked by the range of responses. While we loved to hear about how magical our work was, the vehemently critical feedback about the show was equally informative. It's only in retrospect, through this feedback, that we begin to understand how *The Mists* disrupted the event for attendees, challenging their deeply held conceptions about the natural world.

RED BUTTE GARDENS, A LANDSCAPE

(Liz) I'm standing at the highest point of Red Butte Garden, in the middle of a grassy knoll, the Wasatch front looming behind me. If I walk downhill to the parking lot the Great Salt Lake shimmers in the sun, framed by cars proudly wearing *Protect Wild Utah* bumper stickers. With a stretch of my imagination, I can just glimpse the red rocks of Arches National Park and the deep rifts of Canyonlands to the distant south. Truly, this feels like a protected and beautiful space. It's a relief to be under the heavy Utah sun.

At our first rehearsals, we had to use a map to find our way around the Garden; it's easy to get lost in this sprawling arboretum, a beautiful 'living landscape.' (http://www.redbuttegarden.org/about-us). Conjuring images of rolling hills and oil paintings, 'landscape' evokes idyllic notions of the pastoral intended for enjoyment. The Garden, like other landscapes, is designed to exclude the human from the space (Malpas 6). The natural world is framed and presented for consumption from its paved paths and benches, fixing visitors firmly in the seat of spectator to nature's sensualities. The Garden seems to offer the natural world while actually fixing the viewer outside of it (Chaudhuri 19), replicating the effect of a landscape painting, or fittingly, the proscenium (21).

Utahns are passionate about preserving the natural world for human enjoyment. The state is host to five national parks, forty-five state parks, innumerable wild areas and epic views. We are a hub for environmentalists, conservationists, naturalists, ski racers and rock climbers who all share a love of Wild Utah. This passion for wilderness contributes to a generally uncontested understanding of the environment as pristine, natural and separate from human influence (Cronon 110). Environment depends on being not-human, something out there and away from us. This concept of the environment is not unique to Utah, but rooted in a Western modern worldview that places nature and culture in opposition, marking the natural world separate from, and below, the human realm (Allinson 7,18; Phelan 385). This dominant environmental discourse, with its separation of nature and culture, had a palpable presence in the show. During the focus groups, we were especially aware of this discourse, such as the following clip of a conversation between two staff members.

> "...[In *The Mists*] there's a lot of natural magic happening. And the deer and the Lady of the Lake...it's not like the Jetsons. It's...the natural world, I don't know how to describe it, but I think that tied into the Garden."

> "Yeah, [be]cause outside was where the deer were and inside were the people..." (Focus Group, 12/4/15).

People fit in the indoor parts of the garden, while the deer (animals) should be outdoors. The effect of this conceptual binary that equates inside with human and outside with nature was a certain kind of protectionism of the garden by the staff and volunteers. Even as we were invited in—to make the show, we were cautioned to stay out—of the natural parts of the garden. In deference to their wishes, we choreographed the entire show on grassy lawns and built features of the garden; planters, paths, and benches. Still, in spite of our many admonitions to our performers to "avoid the plants!," someone accidentally stepped on the edge of a flower bed during dress rehearsal. After that, several of the long-established volunteers became concerned about the dancers, notifying us each day with a list of any places where the dancers accidentally transgressed the path. The landscape became a specter hovering over our heads. One dancer commented; "It's odd. Though we are dancing 'in the garden,' we aren't allowed to touch the plants!"

After months of navigating the tensions between our performers' desire to get their hands dirty in the Garden, and the staffs' need for them to be away from the plants, we had imagined a tense relationship between the performers and the space. We were a bit surprised by the focus groups, which revealed affinity and a hint of ownership. The performers affectionately described the Gardens, "It's like we know the space more than anyone else," one stated. Another describing a scene where he canoed through the small lake, spoke as if the lake had been designed just for his needs, stating "That little alcove in the reeds that I found—that was nice. And it was just enough space to turn a canoe around—that was convenient." A third performer spoke about how she was grateful to be able to work within the limitations and rules of the space presented by the Garden staff. For her, this helped her to exist in a land instead of having to create her own land the way that she does in a proscenium work (Focus Group, 12/15/15)

The dancers' sense of the space lingered in their bodies after the show was over. They equated being in the Garden with being their characters, describing how much they missed their characters and the space interchangeably. One character, who played a stag, stated, "If I go [to Red Butte Garden] again, I'll probably want to be in character and be a stag again...I'll probably start to imagine the scenes that I was in..." Later this same artist stated; "...I was so invested [in *The Mists*], I would get lost and forget I was in character...I would make stag noises after we were done when I was just hanging out with my friends." (Focus Group, 12/15/15) The character and the garden melded together in their memory of the event.

One useful frame for this kinesthetic reaction is Phenomenologist Edward Casey's theory of the body as a being-in-place (Casey 413). For Casey, the body and place exist in a dynamic tension in which they continually impact and are impacted by each other. The body goes into place and impacts this place by its presence (414), and the place makes a lasting and permanent impact on the body, causing the sense of the place to persist in the body (415). This persisting sense of place was evidenced by the residual remnants of the character in this performer after the show was over.

The arrival of the audience on opening night was a very dramatic eruption of the human into the landscape, shattering the illusion of Red Butte Garden as an untouched natural place. After opening night, the dancers' relationship to the space expanded to include the audience members. One performer explains; "…when we were rehearsing it was like "how can I use the space?" and highlight things; my body in the space, the space in my body. But then, when there were lots of audience members, [the space] kind of became a secondary concern for me. It became 'who's here? and how can I weave through them?' Like, [awareness of the space] was still a part of the performance, but then the audience was…a huge factor…I would use the plants to hide behind and peer at audience members, but it wasn't like "look at the leaves." (Focus Group, 12/15/15) This dancer went from a focus on a kind of dwelling in space and the usual concerns of ecological and site specific work, to bring the presence of the audience into her awareness.

Another performer, returning to the lake he loved, explained why it was so cool to be in that space, saying; "I found that place behind the reeds where I could canoe…hiding behind those reeds but having it so my canoe barely stuck out. And it was interesting to see people be like 'is there someone out there?' and I felt like a lot of the time it was just a little kid and the parents ignoring them, and [the kid] being like 'No, I really think someone's out there! That was fun.' (Focus Group, 12/15/15) The presence of the kids in the space were part of what gave that place its beauty and resonance for this performer. Though turning the canoe around in that spot was fun and he enjoyed "looking up at the moon," singing and generally doing what his character would do in the water, the presence of the human in the scenery that what caused him to light up when remembering the place.

Like a landscape painting, Red Butte Garden is a place that crosses the worlds of nature, meaning and society (Cresswell 4). The same space filled with natural elements has been constructed by humans, and filled with human built elements; paths, sculptures, benches. This space, a composite of categories of nature and culture, demonstrates that the subject of the landscape—the nature—is not free from cultural coding (Chaudhuri 12). The inclusion of the audience in the performers' understandings of the space caused them to intimately experience a deconstruction of the binary between nature/culture. They experienced the space and knew it intimately, and at the same time they were able to expand their conception of natural space to include the people who populated it during the event.

BUT—WHERE DO I STAND? ON PARENTS, PLAY AND PLACE

(Alysia) I invented immersive theater when I was seven years old. Rounding up a cast of brothers, cousins and pets, I invited an intimate audience of relatives on an interactive and ambulatory dance retelling of *Peter Pan* that traveled through the wilds of my yard, jungle gym, and bedroom (aka secret hideout). As a child, spaces and objects easily transformed to the contours of my imagination; a thicket of sticks became a native hut, a small creek a crocodile infested swamp, a clothesline with sheets the soaring sails of a ship. Oh, I know, I wasn't the first to invent it, children have been doing it for centuries, it's just that we called it "play." Sometimes we did it for an audience and sometimes just for ourselves. The concepts of "site specific," "immersive," "interactive," did not occur to us as novel or groundbreaking forms of theater but simply the way it was done. But as soon as children engage in any kind of formal training, they learn that art happens in boxes. Theater sized boxes and museum sized boxes, television sized boxes and movie screen boxes. I made my first dances in yards, woods, jungle gyms and basements intuitively because it was available, but I learned not to consider these venues once exposed to the opportunity of the stage. Once professional, I spent over a decade making work for the stage and seeing work on stages, coveting specific stages and imagining bigger and bigger stages. Though I saw the occasional site-specific dance or museum piece they failed to grip me and still upheld a formal separation of audience and performer. Even nice site-specific works didn't hold the power or magic of the proscenium stage, appearing as dancers dancing in a small loft, or a gallery with other people's art behind them or frolicking outside.

Garden After Dark attendees follow a consistent pattern each year at the event. Traveling in a counterclockwise route, visitors walk the Garden to see the lights, make some crafts, and depart for home. This annual routine connects visitors to Red Butte Garden in a way that reinforces the Garden as a kind of box for nature; a living landscape to be viewed and enjoyed from a distance. Viewers most readily engaged in the parts of *The Mists* that emphasized and echoed established practices of consuming art from a distance. Our "mini shows" (Focus Group, 12/4/15) that we developed for proscenium style viewing from the paths made it easy for adults to answer their instinctive question of "What do we do—do we stand and watch?" (Focus Group, 12/4/15). These mini-shows were accessible and surprisingly long lasting in people's memories. Those interviewed in our focus group could describe in detail each of these shows that they had seen, even several months after the performance.

The mini-shows fit into the Garden not only because of the way that the Garden was built, but also because of the practiced meanings of *Garden After Dark.* The event route, with its sense of flushing people quickly through the space, was an equal factor with the terrain in determining what was possible in the place. 'Place' is conceptually distinct from 'space' across the arts, humanities and social sciences, indicating not just the topography but also the layers of subjective experience associated with a specific space (see Cachelin and Kloetzel). Places are about experiential, emotional, and ecological connections (Cachelin 6). The meanings (and physical structure) of the place are shaped by the individual and social practices in that place (Cresswell 2, 7). The connections between people and place inform how people act in the space as well as the value that a space holds for people (2).

Staff members considered the event wildly successful, and very challenging for audience members' paradigms. How much an audience member could interact with *The Mists* "depends on how open people are to an experience like that" (Focus Group, 12/4/15) one staff member commented. Another explained, "I think a lot of people who come are repeat visitors, year after year, and it seems like if you were to do something like [*The Mists*] year after year people get more into it. (Focus Group,

12/4/15). This staff member indicates that *The Mists,* a practice which disrupts the established meanings of the Garden could, over time, change the connection that people feel with that place (see Cachelin, Cresswell, Casey).

We thought we were making an adult show at the kid's event, since *The Mists* addresses such adult themes. In actuality, we realized that we were making a kid's show at an adult's event. The hesitance of the adults to engage with *The Mists* caused them to continually hurry their children through the space, while it was the children who were most receptive to the new form when *The Mists* premiered. Always quick to detect the unspoken rules of a new game the kids instinctively followed the performers' lead and began filling in the story. "Follow the evil queen," they piped up at first sight of a severe looking Morgaine La Fey storming away from the mystic Avalon past Guinevere's convent. "She's dead!" they cried when Arthur triumphed over the King Stag. "They're in love," "They broke up," "Over here!" they joined in the action, often as their parents looked bewildered, bothered or impassive. Parents arrived to find the usual path of *Garden After Dark* disrupted. The "real world" of the vendors and food trucks was there, but not as it had been. Overlaying the familiar was the fantastical—pagan priestesses weaving spells into tapestries around trees beckoning the audience to join them, wild stags peering out from behind bushes then extending a hoof awaiting a caress.

(Liz) This morning I woke up with a vision of Dance Team Stags. You know how a really good dance team moves in total unison, down to the placement of their hands? Well, I imagined our stags doing that up and down one of the long pathways. I loved being on a dance team at my alma mater. After years of pre-professional ballet training, the brazen sexuality of our dances was totally liberating; I finally felt powerful and no longer a little girl waiting for a correction from her teacher. This was a Catholic college so we had to hide the sex a little bit. Actually, maybe the sex was in plain sight. During a game with a rival Baptist college, whose students signed a contract saying they wouldn't dance, we performed a hip swinging 80s heavy rock medley. In the middle of Jon Bon Jovi's crescendo, a student heckler actually shouted "Sluts!" at us. When I brought the idea of Dance Team Stags to rehearsal, it was sort of tongue-in-cheek and abashedly. Dance team is not high art, after all! That's just a four-year blank space on my dance CV filled with the male gaze! However, after years of abstract improvisations, the dancers were delighted by its vulgarity. We morphed Dance Team Stags into a traveling phrase, which became the beginning of an entire movement vocabulary for the characters.

Initially, an afterthought built for a battle scene, the stag cast took their bit part and annexed the Garden paths. Cute and uncanny by turn, these elk/deer/wolf being disrupted the practiced landscape of the Garden with their wild howls. Their presence delighted most children and disturbed some parents. A staff member explained; "A lot of people, especially I heard a family—a mom had two girls with her, they loved interacting with the deer. One of the deer made a sound at her and she made it back and they kind of had this back and forth thing going on. But then I also heard, and this was mostly from adults, 'they wouldn't leave me alone' or 'I didn't want to interact...'" (Focus Group, 12/4/15). The uncanny presence of these performers incited some audience members to threats of violence, albeit jokingly. One performer estimated that about a third of the adult audience members made a hunting joke or reference in response to them (Focus Group, 12/15/15). These raw reactions created a strange intimacy between the performer and the audience member. One of the dancers explains; "There's a whole spectrum of...the hunting families and the liberal, vegetarian families...[and] the ones who were totally encouraging of their kids pretending to shoot us. That's a huge part of [audience] identity that you don't normally find out, especially if it's a proscenium work." (Focus Group, 12/15/15) Not only were the performers in physical proximity to the viewers, they were dancing with the cultural identities of the audience.

This immediate and shocking feedback presented an exciting challenge. Because of the intimacy of the audience, performers became passionate about remaining in character, determined to offer each of the guests an experience, if they were open to it. Describing conviction, adaptability, and malleability, the performers spoke compassionately about the audience, saying, "I have to remain really ok with whatever is going to come my way good, bad, or otherwise...understanding that some people just see things differently and some people like different things, and if they don't like it, it's ok." (Focus Group, 12/15/15).

CAMELOT : DANCING TOGETHER

(Liz) Towering gold headpieces and bright red leggings. The eight court dancers in a long line, the mandolin cries overhead. The pace picks up and they stamp and jig in time to the beat. Grabbing the audience by the hand they pull them into the circle and dance. The stags show up at the door with [Le] Fey and priestesses. There must be 100 people crammed into this room dancing right now; kids, adults, cast. The dance party goes on and on, into the following song and beyond, until I finally run out of courtly music and switch to Beyoncé. Now there's only a few audience members (mostly my thesis committee and their families) and even the cast members themselves trickle away to change into street clothes and remove their makeup.

This was really the only way that *The Mists* could finally end—by totally breaking down the boundaries between performer/audience, inside/outside, high art/low art, human/stag. Even before this evening, audience members would usually stop and stay at Camelot with the courts people, the last stop in the Gardens before exiting the event, for extended stretches of time. After their long journey through *Garden After Dark*, this pause was a surrender to the magic of *The Mists*. Camelot became a liminal place, affording the attendees a chance to transition from the mystical realms of Avalon back to the inside of their Subaru Foresters.

Whether the audience paused at one mini-show, took a moment to pet a stag, or experienced nothing at all, the production afforded a labyrinth in which one might get lost, a rare opportunity. Rebecca Solsnit says; "The question then is how to get lost. Never to get lost is not to live, not to know how to get lost brings you to, destruction and to the terra incognita in between lies the life of discovery." (14) It was not just the audience members who got chance lost in *The Mists,* but we, the cast and choreographers, as well. For those of us inside of the production *The Mists* became our own field guide to getting lost; a chance to find anew the curiosity and playfulness for dance that inspired each of us to join this field in the first place. This journey of discovery was a disruption and expansion of the landscape, an intimate experience of a sometimes unaccepting and violent audience, and a radically redefined theatrical event in Salt Lake City.

BIBLIOGRAPHY

Allinson, Jodie. "Training Strategies for Performance and Landscape: Resisting the Late-capitalist Metaphor of Environment as Consumable Resource." *Theatre, Dance and Performance Training* 5, No. 1 (2014): 4–4.

Cachelin, Adrienne, Jeff Rose, and Danya Rumore. "Leveraging Place and Community for Critical Sustainability Education: The Promise of Participatory Action Research," *Journal of Sustainability Education,* (publication in process, 2016).

Casey, Edward S. "Body, self and landscape: A Geophilosophical Inquiry into the Place-World." in *Textures of Place: Exploring Humanist Geographies,* edited by Paul Adams, Steven Hoelscher, and Karen Till, 403–419. Minneapolis: University of Minnesota Press, 2001.

Chaudhuri, Una. "Land/scape/theory." In *Land/Scape/Theater*, edited by Una Chaudhuri and Elinor Fuchs, 11–29. Ann Arbor: University of Michigan Press, 2002.

Cronon, William. "The Trouble with Wilderness; or Getting Back to the Wrong Nature." In *Ecocriticism, The Essential Reader,* edited by Ken Hiltner, 102–119. New York: Routledge, 2015.

Habel, Shana L. "History of the Modern Dance Program at the University of Utah 1968–1989" Masters Thesis. Salt Lake City: University of Utah Press, 2010.

Kloetzel, Melanie. "Site-Specific Dance in a Corporate Landscape." *New Theatre Quarterly,* 26, No. 2 (2010): 133–144.

Malpas, Jeff. "Place and the Problem of Landscape." In *The Place of Landscape: Concepts, Contexts, Studies,* 3–25. Cambridge: The MIT Press, 2011.

Phelan, Shane. "Intimate Distance: The Dislocation of Nature in Modernity." *The Western Political Quarterly* 45, No 2 (1992): 385–342.

"Place," Tim Cresswell. Retrieved January 10, 2016. http://booksite.elsevier.com /brochures/hugy/SampleContent/Place.pdf

Solnit, Rebecca. *A Field Guide to Getting Lost.* New York: Penguin Group, 2005.

The Mists performer focus group. December 15, 2015. The University of Utah Marriott Library.

Red Butte Garden, *Garden After Dark* staff focus group. December 4, 2015. Red Butte Gardens.

CHAPTER 4

Game/Play: The Five Conceptual Planes of Punchdrunk's *Sleep No More*

Sara Thiel

> [G]ame spaces evoke narratives because the player is making sense of them in order to engage with them. Through a comprehension of signs and interaction with them, the player generates new. meaning[51].

In 2011, Punchdrunk and Emursive transformed three Chelsea, Manhattan warehouses into what Ben Brantley calls a "1930s pleasure palace."[52] This "pleasure palace," otherwise known as the McKittrick Hotel, is the home of *Sleep No More*, an interactive promenade performance directed by Felix Barrett and Maxine Doyle. Punchdrunk's commercially and critically successful production invites audiences to discover the history of a mysterious hotel through the lens of William Shakespeare's *Macbeth*.[53] *Sleep No More* was initially set to run in New York from February to May 2011; the run has been extended several times with no end in sight, due to high public demand.[54] If adaptations of Shakespeare's works are a "cultural barometer for the historically contingent process of adaptation," as Julie Sanders argues, what can the popularity of this intertextual riff on Shakespeare's ill-fated Scottish King tell us about contemporary American audiences?[55] What can *Sleep No More*'s success help us understand about why interactive performance appeals to audiences steeped in digital entertainment? The overwhelmingly enthusiastic response to Punchdrunk's distinctive mode of adapting Shakespeare's work and engaging spectators reveals the need to re-examine the ways in which contemporary theatre audiences desire to take in live performance.

In this chapter, I argue the popularity of *Sleep No More* stems from the success of a similar phenomenon: dynamic story-based video games. According to a 2015 report by the Entertainment Software Association, 42% of Americans play video games

---

[51] Michael Nitsche, Video Game Space: Image, Play, and Structure in 3D Game Worlds (Cambridge, MA: MIT Press, 2008), 3.

[52] Ben Brantley, "Shakespeare Slept Here, Albeit Fitfully," The New York Times, 13 April 2011. Accessed 21 December 2015, http://www.nytimes.com/2011/04/14/theater/reviews/sleep-no-more-is-a-macbeth-in-a-hotel-review.html?_r=0.

[53] Sleep No More's awards include: a Drama Desk Award for Unique Theatrical Experience and a Special Citation for Design and Choreography at the Obie Awards, both in 2011.

[54] "Current Shows: Sleep No More-NYC," Punchdrunk, accessed December 18, 2015, http://punchdrunk.com/current-shows.

[55] Julie Sanders, Adaptation and Appropriation (New York: Routledge, 2006), 21.

three or more hours per week; four out of five households own a device used to play video games.[56] *Sleep No More* appeals to a generation of audiences raised on interactive, immersive, story-based video games in which the choices one makes affect the attributes of one's character and the outcome of the story itself.[57] One can see this method of storytelling most readily in games such as: BioWare's *Mass Effect* and *Dragon Age* multi-part series (2007–2016 and 2009–2014, respectively), Quantic Dream's *Heavy Rain* (2010), and even recently digitized tabletop games such as *Dungeons and Dragons* (first released in 1974).[58] Similar to these games, with their myriad of dynamic choices and consequences, the *Sleep No More* playgoer/game player makes sense of the world as she moves through the dynamic, immersive space.

I suggest that, like a video game, the success of *Sleep No More* is contingent upon the interaction between the playgoer and the multi-layered playing space. Only through experiencing and interacting with the "in-game" environment does the audience come to create meaning and construct the play (or game's) narrative. In so doing, the audience becomes invested in the game/play by physically participating in the act of storytelling and meaning making.[59] Punchdrunk has created a physically engaging theatre experience, accessible because of its similarities to a familiar digital medium.

Analyzing the ways in which *Sleep No More* playgoers create meaning "in-game," this essay adapts Michael Nitsche's "Five Conceptual Planes" from his 2008 theoretical study of three-dimensional video game spaces.[60] Nitsche's work is appropriate for the purposes of this study, as his comprehensive and interdisciplinary approach asks the reader to consider the ways in which a game's sound, architectural, and cinematic design effect the player's ability to make sense of the in-game world. Similarly, *Sleep No More* interweaves media in order to create holistic environment for the spectator.

In part one, I look to the "play space" of the performance. While Nitsche defines "play space" as the physical site wherein "the player and the video game hardware" exist, I introduce *Sleep No More*'s playing space, including the many levels of acclimation each spectator endures before entering the performance. Next, I examine *Sleep No More*'s "rule-based space" in which audiences are simultaneously free to explore, but also restricted in a number of key ways throughout the duration of the play. Part three explores the design of *Sleep No More*: the "mediated space" in which the audience aesthetically engages the play. The fourth part looks to the "fictional space," or the "space 'imagined' by players from their comprehension of the available

---

[56] Entertainment Software Administration, The 2015 Essential Facts About the Computer and Video Game Industry, April 2015, accessed December 21, 2015, *http://www.theesa.com/wp-content/uploads/2015/%2004/ESA-Essential-Facts-2015.pdf*, 2.

[57] According to the same 2015 ESA report 74% of game players are over the age of 18; 54% are over the age of 35.

[58] Dungeons and Dragons is now in its fifth edition as of 2014 and was published as a MMORPG in 2006.

[59] While Sleep No More is immersive, in that audience members can, and do, become part of the action, they are not agents of change within the world of the play. While Punchdrunk strives to give the audience member the agency to play and discover, they do not give so much agency as to allow the audience to change the events of the play, only their own perception of it.

[60] See: Michael Nitsche, Video Game Space: Image, Play, and Structure in 3D Game Worlds (Cambridge, MA: MIT Press, 2008), 1–21.

images," by analyzing *Sleep No More* as a work of adaptation.[61] Finally, I analyze *Sleep No More*'s "social space" by examining the broad audience base to which this play appeals, as well as the myriad of audience interactions that occur in and out-of-game. Using Nitsche's "Five Conceptual Planes" to analyze *Sleep No More*, I argue Punchdrunk owes its commercial success to its interactive video game model that appeals to a broad base of playgoers/game players.

I. PLAY SPACE: THE HOTEL

Approaching *Sleep No More*'s performance space, one might miss the entire play if not for the line down the block outside of a seemingly abandoned warehouse. There are no markers aside from a small brass plaque posted by the main entrance identifying the building, which cannot be read from the street. Taxicabs pull up curbside, dumping off bewildered patrons who wonder if they have the correct address. Upon entering the warehouse, the audience member is transported to a 1930s hotel; this is the McKittrick. Upon check-in, the front desk clerk hands over the room key: a playing card from a standard deck. The clerk gives the guest instructions to ascend a small flight of stairs and follow the corridor. This hallway, which seems to go on for miles, twisting and turning, intentionally disorients guests, forcing them to lose all sense of direction. A soft jazz tune floats from somewhere in the distance and suddenly a shock of red comes into view through a pair of split curtains. On the other side of those curtains, the world transforms in to a Prohibition-era speakeasy: the Manderley bar.

The bar is a pre-show performance of sorts, acting as a "decompression chamber" that allows the audience "to acclimatize to the world before being set free in it," as Barrett describes it.[62] The audience becomes accustomed to the environment of the bar, which creates a smoother transition into the world of the performance. As hotel guests belly up to the bar, they are invited to purchase an old-fashioned cocktail and enjoy the entertainment: a three-piece jazz band. After a few minutes, the band takes a break from their set as the emcee, a tall thin man in a tuxedo, approaches the microphone. He calls for everyone with an ace playing card to enter the hotel. Guests holding those "keys" disappear through a hidden door in the corner of the bar. This process continues throughout the rest of the evening. Every fifteen minutes the emcee calls for the twos, threes, and so forth, until all guests have entered the hotel.

Once through the door, guests find themselves inside what appears to be an antechamber. Everyone receives a white plastic Venetian-style mask, which they are instructed to wear throughout the duration of their stay at the McKittrick. While donning their masks, the group waits for an elevator to arrive; when it does, a lanky, gaunt bellhop welcomes the group into a large industrial lift. At this point, the playgoer/game player has left the decompression chamber and enters the game/play's tutorial.

---

[61] Nitsche, Video Game Spaces, 16.
[62] Machon, (Syn)aesthetics, 90–1.

II. RULE-BASED SPACE: THE TUTORIAL

Michael Nitsche defines the "rule-based space" as that which is limited "by the code, the data, and hardware restrictions."[63] For the purposes of my argument, I adapt Nitsche's concept of the "rule-based space" to include the "given circumstances" of the performance—the rules by which interaction with the physical world is governed. These rules are delivered in the form of a "tutorial," similar to that of a complex video game wherein the player is taught, in-game, how to interact with the space. The tutorial is a point of acclimation to the game space: players learn the object of the game, how to perform actions such as run, jump, or shoot, and investigate the new world in which they are presently immersed. Similarly, the elevator ride acts as *Sleep No More*'s official "tutorial," empowering audience members to become makers of meaning during the performance, while keeping in mind the limitations of the playing space.

Comparable to the way in which a video game player is limited by the hardware on which the game is played (PC, Xbox, PlayStation, etc.), or the game developer's coding, *Sleep No* More's audience members are faced with similar restrictions: they are verbally instructed to remain silent while wearing their mask throughout the entire performance. Other than that, each spectator is free to explore the space in whatever way she chooses. However, if an audience member attempts to engage with the space, audience, or actors in some way that is not permissible, the bellhop assures the group a black-masked stagehand will emerge from the darkness and instruct the "player" accordingly.

These stagehands have a similar function to in-game customer support staff for a massively multiplayer online role-playing game (MMORPG) such as Blizzard's *World of Warcraft*.[64] While many of these in-game staff members work retroactively to resolve problems or player grievances, some may "patrol" the game, looking to correct those who are cheating or harassing other players. Most MMORPG players never recognize the presence of these "game masters"; similarly, most *Sleep No More* audience members take no notice of these sable-clad stagehands who direct players throughout the world of the play while maintaining the game/play's physical boundaries. These people move in the shadows of the playing space, acting as moving roadblocks for audience members where necessary, without interrupting the carefully choreographed and designed flow of the play. While there are certainly constraints, limits, and borders to the game map and the playing space, the spectator is nevertheless encouraged to explore the detail-rich world in order to progress the story's plot. In this way, *Sleep No More*'s unfolds uniquely for each playgoer.

---

[63] Nitsche, Video Game Spaces, 16.

[64] Blizzard describes their own game masters as those who: "wait in the shadows, poised to help when things in your Blizzard gaming experience go awry, and they're available 24 hours a day" ("What Does a Game Master Really Do?" World of Warcraft, accessed December 21, 2015, *http://us.battle.net/wow/en/blog* /8501406/what-does-a-game-master-really-do-1-22-2013).

III. Mediated Space: The Material World

Sleep No More takes place inside three disused Chelsea warehouses made to look like a 1930s Hitchcock-esque Inverness. This is the "mediated space," which "consists of all the output the system can provide in order to present the rule-based game universe to the player."[65] In other words: if the "rule-based space" is that which is constructed by an agreement between players and playmakers to stay within the physical borders of the performance, the "mediated space" is the aesthetic form the performance takes. Considering Nitsche's definition dramaturgically, the "mediated space" is the installation, as well as the ways in which audience members move through space while interacting with the material world of the play.

Once inside the performance space, the spectator is set free to investigate the installation and seek out the story for herself. Audience members are given no explicit instructions or narrative to follow other than the initial tutorial guidelines. Nevertheless, Barrett and Doyle curated the performance space in order to guide the audience through the story, using sound, light, and architecture strategically, careful to avoid dictating individual journeys.[66] Like the design of a complex game map, the player is encouraged to experience the space and story at her own pace while taking cues from the space's design. For example, in the *Mass Effect* trilogy, players move about The Citadel, a central in-game hub with a detail-rich map. Each section of the Citadel houses various populations of non-player-controlled characters. Players explore the Citadel and speak to these characters, accepting quests that help advance the game's plot. Similarly, *Sleep No More* audience members explore the thoroughness of each room's unique design, such as the hospital, the taxidermist, or the Macbeth's home, and follow different characters on quests to learn the details of the McKittrick's inhabitants.

Although audience members can follow a menagerie of characters throughout the hotel, they are also free to carefully inspect the detail-rich installation room-by-room if they so choose. Spectators can open crisp handwritten letters or inspect the antique contents of private closets; they can sit and read one of the dusty books on the shelf; they can listen to a record on a Victrola if they so desire. Similar to the ways in which players of *Fallout*, a long-running survival game series, search buildings for spare loot and information about the game's plot, many *Sleep No More* audience members spend the majority of their time digging through trunks and closets to fully comprehend the extensiveness of the installation. In so doing, playgoers engage with the immersive 1930s design in a tactile and olfactory, rather than merely a visual or aural way.[67]

---

[65] Nitsche, Video Game Design, 16.

[66] Maxine Doyle notes she and Barrett have included many "signifiers in place to lead the audience, to give them more clues, not to follow a narrative but in a really simple way to indicate where action is going to happen or where there's going to be some big shift. Whether that's through lighting changes or music changes, using all the conventions you find in theatre but using them to give the audience cues so that there is some information to help them crack the puzzle. It's all visceral and emotional; we don't really give them any intellectual clues" (Machon, (Syn)aesthetics, 91).

[67] Felix Barrett founded Punchdrunk in 2000 in an effort to create theatre that empowered audiences to make interpretive decisions about the performance while determining the nature of their physical experience at the theatre When Maxine Doyle, co-director and choreographer of Sleep No More, joined Punchdrunk in 2003, the company began producing the kind of work for which it has become well known. Coming from a background in dance, Doyle's central frustration with performing on a proscenium stage is that the dance felt too distant from the audience, rather than immediate and visceral. Barrett and Doyle's

While the immersive quality of *Sleep No More* draws many spectators into the world of the play aesthetically, there are nevertheless an entire host of literary and cultural echoes that are not explicitly referenced during the production. It is only through understanding *Sleep No More* as an adaptation that we can fully comprehend the ways in which audiences make sense of the play's story. *Sleep No More*'s film noir World War II aesthetic, paired with the game playing experience of the performance, collide within the cultural memory of the audience as they attempt to untangle the McKittrick's history.

IV. FICTIONAL SPACE: THE ADAPTATION

Sleep No More is an adaptation of Shakespeare's *Macbeth* and Daphne du Maurier's *Rebecca*. This interactive and adaptive performance not only offers audience members the opportunity to engage with the playing, rule-based, and mediated spaces of the play, but also imaginatively engage with the multi-layered fictional world as well. Nitsche's defines "fictional space" as that which lives in the player's imagination based on information provided by the mediated space. For the purposes of this essay, I adapt the idea of the "fictional" or "imagined" space to be the variety of source texts that ghost *Sleep No More*.[68] Throughout Punchdrunk's performance, theatrical, literary, and historical worlds interweave, intertwine, and collide in a mash-up of cultural echoes.

Despite the interactive and viscerally evocative nature of *Sleep No More*, W.B. Worthen calls the play "'text-based' in a surprisingly imaginative, surprisingly literal way."[69] Taking *Rebecca*, a Gothic novel, and *Macbeth*, a Jacobean drama, as its central sources, *Sleep No More* interweaves these texts, each with a rich literary and performance history of their own. *Rebecca* is Daphne du Maurier's 1938 reworking of Charlotte Brontë's 1847 novel, *Jane Eyre*. Since its initial publication, the novel has undergone many adaptations and re-workings of its own, including Alfred Hitchcock's 1940 Academy Award winning film starring Laurence Olivier. Hitchcock's adaptation, along with the compositions of Bernard Herrmann, inspired the environment, atmosphere, and design for *Sleep No More*.[70]

---

collaboration allowed them to focus on storytelling through gesture and physical expression, free from the confines of the proscenium (Machon, (Syn)aesthetics, 89–90). Working toward audience empowerment and performer proximity to bring a unique experience to both actors and spectators, Punchdrunk "rejects the passive obedience usually expected of audience members," so that boundaries between spectator and performer are constantly in flux ("Company," Punchdrunk, accessed 14 September 2015, *http:// punchdrunk.com/company*).

[68] Marvin Carlson defines "ghosting" as a fundamental characteristic of live performance because of the ways in which memory is so deeply connected to embodied experience (6–8). Discussing site-specific performances, Carlson suggests theatricalized spaces simultaneously project ghostings of their non-theatrical historical associations (13;131–64). Marvin Carlson, The Haunted Stage: The Theatre as Memory Machine, (Ann Arbor, MI: The University of Michigan Press, 2003), 13.

[69] W.B. Worthen, Shakespeare Performance Studies (Cambridge: Cambridge University Press, 2014), 130.

[70] While Herrmann composed music for many Hitchcock films, he did not write Rebecca's score.

While *Sleep No More* employs the entire dramatic arc of *Macbeth*, along with most of the play's central characters, Barrett and Doyle added a considerable number of characters and spaces more suited to du Maurier's world.[71] Barrett and Doyle weave these sources and their precursors together in such a way that *Sleep No More* becomes a complex intertextual pastiche.

Barrett and Doyle's scenic installation is also ghosted by a number of cultural and historical echoes simultaneously. The spectral figures that populate *Sleep No More* make audiences feel as though they intrude upon a private haunted world. Each room carries its own set of signifiers, imparting various ghosting effects upon the audience. The historical background of the bloody, gruesome trauma of World War II echoes the events of the play, especially in the hauntingly empty hospital ward: the dead have awoken from their beds and gone for a stroll about the hotel. The bloodied sheets of the Macduff family home leave the audience with the uneasy feeling of entering a horrific homicide in a film noir murder mystery. The lively dance floor and free-flowing liquor in the ballroom is reminiscent of a gathering in F. Scott Fitzgerald's West Egg. One feels like Nick Carraway of *The Great Gatsby*: a voyeuristic outsider looking in at the events unfolding before him. Hecate's rave-like prophecy session calls to mind the history of the former Chelsea clubs littered throughout the area, many of which were condemned by New York police in 2010 as safe-havens for drug dealers.[72]

Perhaps most interestingly, many video game players, bloggers, and critics have drawn comparisons between the experience of *Sleep No More* and similarly structured story-based such as the first two installments of 2K Games' *BioShock* series (2007–2013).[73] These survival horror games, first-person shooters inspired by Ayn Rand's Objectivist philosophy, are set in a frightening underwater dystopia of human mutation and lavish Art Deco design. The common comparisons between *Sleep No More* and games such as *Bioshock* and *Shadowgate* (1987) stem from *Sleep No More*'s interactive performance style as well as its Hitchcockian design aesthetic.[74]

While the mediated experience of *Sleep No More* can be intimidating to spectators without any experience in this kind of interactive performance, audiences are not thrown into the wild without a map. Rather, they find themselves dropped into the performance of a play adapted from Shakespeare, anchored in a design world inspired by the cinematic styling of Alfred Hitchcock, utilizing an interactive interface similar to that of video role-playing and survival games. Barrett and Doyle weave all of these styles together in the hopes that this immersive experience appeals to all individual spectators in a myriad of ways.

---

[71] For example, the Manderley bar is named after the estate in du Maurier's novel. Audience members are also invited to purchase an "add-on" to their ticket called "SLEEP NO MORE as Maximilian's Guest." Maximilian, of course, is the "proprietor" of the McKittrick Hotel, named for du Maurier's character in *Rebecca* (played by Olivier in the Hitchcock film).

[72] Diane Cardwell, "Police Close Sister Clubs, M2 and Pink, in Chelsea," The New York Times, April 19 2010, accessed December 21, 2015, http://www.nytimes.com/2010/04/20/nyregion/20club.html.

[73] Cyriaque Lamar, "Sleep No More=LARP+Shakespeare+ Absinthe+ Orgy Masks," io9, November 13 2011, accessed December 10 2015, *http://io9.com/5859100/sleep-no-more--larp-%252B-shakespeare-%252B-absinthe-%252B-orgy-masks*.

[74] ibid.

V. Social Space: The Audience

In the final section of the chapter, I explore the ways in which Barrett and Doyle's distinct form of storytelling engages players in the "social space," defined by Nitsche as interaction among players in-game.[75] While Nitsche's understanding of "social space" applies to MMOs, such as *World of Warcraft* or *Battlefield*, the "social space" of *Sleep No More* is the world inhabited and controlled by the play-going game players outside the actual game/play space. Using Richard A. Bartle's taxonomy of game players in order to explore the ways in which Barrett and Doyle's immersive environment appeals to a broad play going/game playing base, I argue *Sleep No More* is a commercial success not only because it appeals to spectators on multiple sensory levels, but also because of the ways it relocates the social space.[76]

According to Bartle's taxonomy there are four broad types of game players: Socializers, Achievers, Explorers, and Killers. Socializers are those "for whom the greatest reward is interacting with other people, through the medium of the virtual world."[77] One would think Socializers would not find *Sleep No More* to be an enjoyable experience considering spectators are barred from verbally engaging during the play. What's more, it is difficult for groups or pairs to remain together throughout the course of a performance. Due to this aspect of the performance, Michael Billington has criticized Punchdrunk for robbing the theatre of its sense of community, placing emphasis on the individual journey.[78] What Billington fails to note is that the communal experience, if absent "in-game," takes place once the play has concluded in person and online.

After the play ends, Socializers re-convene in the Manderley bar to piece their experience together, learning what they missed and sharing what they discovered. One can hear similar conversations happening between individuals who play through the *Mass Effect* trilogy as they attempt to learn how the in-game choices of their friends altered gameplay, resulting in a fundamentally different gaming experience. Similarly, Socializers who attend *Sleep No More* alone inevitably find themselves on their phones afterward: calling, texting, Facebooking, Tweeting, Instagramming, and Snapchatting friends who have been to the show, or perhaps inviting those who have not.[79] While individuals may not be sharing the play going experience in the moment, a sense of community remains and is even expanded upon due to the wide reach of social networking platforms. Admittedly, inside the McKittrick Hotel, the focus is on the individual journey; however, the communal experience is merely re-located so that it occurs outside the performance space, not unlike single-players role-playing games.

Maxine Doyle notes: you "don't have to be an experienced theatregoer to play the game [because *Sleep No More*] is multidimensional in terms of what people can tune into"; considering Bartle's three remaining player types, it becomes clear the

---

[75] Nitsche, Video Game Spaces, 16.

[76] Richard A. Bartle, Designing Virtual Worlds (San Francisco, CA: New Riders, 2003), 130.

[77] Bartle, Designing Virtual Worlds,130.

[78] Michael Billington, "The Masque of the Red Death," The Guardian, 4 October 2007, accessed December 2015, *http://www.theguardian.com/ stage/2007/oct/04/theatre*.

[79] The hashtag #sleepnomorenyc is used on Twitter by past and prospective audience members looking to share information about their experiences.

commercial success of an interactive play like *Sleep No More* is due, in part, to its facility in engaging multiple playing styles.[80] Achievers are those who like to complete "defined goals, thereby progressing their character through the world's built-in ranking system."[81] While *Sleep No More* has no official ranking system or list of accomplishments, the Achiever playgoer/game player aims to see every room, scene, and character while witnessing every plot point throughout the duration of the performance. Bartle's third player type is the Explorer, whose "joy is in the discovery."[82] For this player, "increasing their knowledge about the way the virtual world works" fulfills their in-game desires.[83] As I have discussed above, there are a plethora of rooms, characters, and minute details for these Explorers to find throughout the entire performance. In this way, *Sleep No More* as a simultaneously staged and immersive installation is an ideal performance experience for the Explorer. Finally, Killers are those who seek to "dominate others" in-game.[84] For a performance like *Sleep No More*, this may mean Killers push their way to the front of every crowd in order to get the best view of the action, or they may sprint through the labyrinthine halls of the McKittrick in order to "best" fellow players. Killers are always looking for ways to put themselves ahead of the pack, literally and figuratively.

Sleep No More's commercial success relies largely on its appeal to Bartle's four broadly defined player types, who are each likely to become repeat ticket buyers for varying reasons.[85] The Achiever, interested in "completing" the story, may attend the play several times in order to make certain they have witnessed everything there is to see. Socializers bring friends with them in order to broaden the social sphere of the game while Explorers return hoping to discover more about the world, the story, and the rich details that make up the immersive installation. Part of the joy for the Killer is to dominate other players, so they bring uninitiated guests with them for their repeat performance viewings. Similar to the ways in which complex story-based possess what players call "re-play value," the re-watch value of *Sleep No More* to a broad range of playgoers/game players ultimately leads to its commercial viability.[86]

---

[80] Machon, (Syn) Aesthetics, 92.

[81] Bartle, Designing Virtual Worlds, 130.

[82] ibid

[83] ibid.

[84] ibid.

[85] Sleep No More's financial viability can be inferred from its high rate of sold-out performances along with its large capacity and ticket prices. In the second half of December 2015 alone, over 50 percent of the performances were sold out, not including the New Year's Eve Masquerade performance. With a nightly capacity of 300–500 "guests," and ticket prices ranging from $80–$120 (before special "add-ons" like a champagne table), Sleep No More continues to prove a worthwhile investment for Sleep No More's production company, Emursive. Founded in order to fund Sleep No More's New York production, Emursive has reportedly set records as the "highest costing Off-Broadway show in history at somewhere between the $5 and $10 million dollar mark," according to a 2014 Forbes report. Hollie Slade, "Meet Emursive, The Company Behind 'Sleep No More,' The Off-Broadway Production That's Been Sold Out for Three Years," Forbes, March 19, 2014, access December 18, 2015, *http://www.forbes.com /%20sites/hollieslade/2014/03/19/meet-emursive-the-company-behind-sleep-no-more-the-off-broadway-production-thats-been-sold-out-for-three-years/*

[86] After the initial visit to the McKittrick Hotel, patrons are consistently invited back to rediscover the hotel or, perhaps, investigate what they may have missed during their last visit. Part of the temptation for repeat ticket buyers is the fact Punchdrunk continues to add new elements to the production itself. For example, the hotel proprietor, "Maximilian," sent a telegram invite out for an April Fool's Day "remix" performance of the play. The telegram specified that first time guests were not permitted to join this event; only Sleep

VI. CONCLUSION: THE CRITICS

With four year's worth of extended performances in New York, the commercial and critical success of Punchdrunk's *Macbeth* adaptation tells us contemporary audiences, steeped in digital technology, desire a participatory play-going experience as well. *Sleep No More* finds its success with audiences searching for new and innovative ways to engage with Shakespeare, live performance, and one another. As such, an interactive performance like *Sleep No More* points to the need for us to reconsider the seemingly impermeable boundaries between "game playing" and "play-going" in the digital age.

No More veterans were able to rediscover the performance all over again. This invitation is compelling to all four of Bartle's player types. The e-mail went out on 16 March 2012, and the performance was sold-out within days.

CHAPTER 5

From Space to Place: The Audience Journey in Anu Productions 'The Boys of Foley Street'

Pamela McQueen

In this article, I analyze my audience research findings from Anu Productions' *The Boys of Foley Street* (BOFS), in terms of the philosophies of space of Henri Lefebvre, Doreen Massey, and Gaston Bachelard, as well as Jacques Rancière's theory of spectatorship. The performance stages historical social interactions superimposed upon a current architecture. It negotiates what Lefebvre calls representations of space, namely the city planners' conceptualization of space in the most recent public regeneration of Foley Street. The performance, by bringing audience and actor out onto the streets, challenges the city planners regenerated abstraction of urban space in a performative spatial practice. This article will map the audience immersion in the performance as a journey of location engagement from Lefebvrian space to what Massey terms a "place event." This analysis will show that through spatial practice, the representational space imposed on Foley street by, variously, moralists and urban planners, is opened up, negotiated and reinterpreted. This ultimately changes audiences' representations of space, that is to say, their imaginative relationships with this socially deprived area of Dublin. Brian Singleton, in writing of his own audience experience, discusses how the performance "did generate spectral discourse on the ghosting of the sites" (35). He is also very clear that the performance did not privilege performance on these sites over community usage and that "while all of the sites were in public ownership, not all...could be layered in new meaning" (36). My research explores the interaction of the audience with the nature and functions of these pre-existing sites that frame their participative engagement in the performance.

Anu Productions grew from Louise Lowe's directing work with community theatre and developed into a collective that practices site-specific performance in north inner city Dublin. Its performance style uses the spatial practices of a community in their specific location to articulate a lived history of a place. As a result, time is a shifting feature in the performances. Social mores and physical behaviours of times past are performed with contemporary costume and language. Narrative elements of character and dialogue are generated out of archival material of community members' oral history. BOFS is the third part of a larger Monto Cycle of site specific and immersive performances, much of the material for which drawn from the North Inner City Folklore Project. The title of the performance is taken from an iconic live radio interview about the Boot Boys of Foley Street that was broadcast in

1979. For this production, the transcript was re-recorded by teenagers currently living in the area (personal interview, 2012).

The audience coming to an Anu performance, informed by the box office of the nature of the event, has an expectation of an immersive experience. Anu performers develop their rhythms and time the pace of the show to encourage and elicit an active physical and vocal response from the audience. During BOFS the audience member will be kissed, danced with, fed, held hands with, hugged and repeatedly asked questions. In close proximity to the actors at all time, the Anu audience experience is active on both a physical sensual level of touch and smell, whilst also stimulating rapid cognitive shifts of narrative construction as they are sped through seemingly unrelated ubiquitous images of "everyday" life on Foley Street.

THE SOCIAL PRODUCTION OF FOLEY STREET

Lefebvre categorises three types of space as representations of space, spatial practice and representational space. In the audience interviewees' vivid post show memories of their interactive engagement with physical and social behaviours, Foley St. becomes a space "directly lived through its associated images and symbols" (39). For Lefebvre, space is "social morphology: it is to lived experience what form itself is to the living organism, and just as intimately bound up with function and structure" (94).

But the audience does not start with this relationship to Foley Street. Susan Bennett has pointed out the audience experience of performance starts long before the show begins in the engagement of expectations (86–125). Going to Foley Street, one aspect of audiences' expectation is their ideational or imagined expectation of that space as a representational space. Representational space is space "as directly lived through its associated images and symbols" (39). This is the space created in imagination.

The eight participants in the study all filled out pre-show questionnaires indicating their experience of Foley St. and its surrounds was either a). none; b). an occasional cut through driving or cycling to work; or c). going to an exhibition or rehearsal space at the Arts Lab. There was, however, recognition of the historical name of the area as the Monto, a red-light district and latterly an area of social housing in what is termed corporation flats. In fact, some of the participants who had experienced violence in different socially deprived areas of similar architecture, such as the corporation style flats, brought these experiences up in pre-show questionnaires and post show interviews. In one pre-show questionnaire, the respondent described her reaction to the area of social housing on Railway Street as carrying 'the social stigma associated with it, I was mugged by a group of young boys near corporation flats in Smithfield' (Interviewee B). In another pre-show questionnaire, a respondent equated Foley Street to other deprived sections of the city "you know, I've lived in rough areas and been broken into by junkies six times" (Interviewee C). Clearly, the representational space carried specific connotations of criminality or illicit behaviours for the audience before they even arrived at The Lab on Foley St. to pick up their headphones to hear the audio that starts the show. The audience all carried, to some degree, a state of wary nervous tension in terms of what could happen on these streets, along with the sense of excited expectation that goes with any performance. One woman recalled:

I actually had my back to the wall because I said if I have my back to the wall nobody can come up behind me. So, I was going I just wanted to be able to see everything (Interviewee E).

As another example, the man who had previously referenced the house break-ins by junkies talked about the start as follows:

On the headset and you're thinking…I genuinely thought at any time I was waiting for something to go wrong. I had a tension from the off and eh the surprises and the disorientation really of the different, like the scrapping lads, the surrounds and I saw a lot of guys in the park with drink (Interviewee C).

These imaginings of Foley St. loaded with trepidation are incipient before the performance proper begins. This may reflect a wary approach of a mainly middle or lower middle class audience (according to biographical markers on the pre-show questionnaire) entering a low income working class neighbourhood.

In terms of social morphology, this perceptual class barrier in the audience representations of Foley St. affects the lived experience of this space. Anu, to create immersive participative actions with the audience, will have to counter and overcome defensive structures of social behaviours brought by the audience to the production.

REPRESENTATIONS OF FOLEY STREET

These representational spaces informed the audiences initial engagement with the performance but the physical space they are standing and walking through in the first half of *Boys of Foley Street* is what Le Febvre would term a representation of space. Representations of space are the conceptualized spaces of planners, architects and urbanists. These are the dominant space in any society and tend towards organization through a system of verbal signs that requires intellectual engagement by the user (Lefebvre 390). These are often homogenized and controlled spaces. This is a type of dominated space where an insertion of technology, for example an architectural feature, has utterly redefined that space (164). Representations of space are part of the history of ideologies, and by studying the changing plans of a space over time the history of ideologies can be studied (116).

The first three plays of the Monto Cycle, *World's End Lane*, *Laundry* and *The Boys of Foley Street*, could be said to chart several generations of ideologies of planners in representations of space. World's End Lane is the name of the main street through the red-light district of Dublin in the 1700–1800 hundreds. The street became Montgomery Street in the eighteenth century in honour of the maiden name of the wife of the head of the Gardiner family. The Gardiners were the Anglo-Irish ascendancy family that planned and built the Georgian quarter at the heart of north Dublin. Montgomery St. gave its name to "the Monto," the notorious red light district of the nineteenth century (Murphy 30–31). In 1905, the nationalist Dublin Corporation renamed Montgomery St. as Foley St. in an effort to diffuse the associations of the notorious Monto name (Lanigan 185–186). Post Irish independence, a lay section of the Catholic Church led a campaign to clear the area of prostitutes, many of who ended up in the Magdalene Laundry. The brothels were knocked down and regenerated as state social housing of flat complexes during the tenement house clearances of the nineteen-fifties ("An Phoblacht," 2002). The cross-street Corporation Street was renamed James Joyce Street in the nineteen-nineties when the majority of the council flats, now synonymous with crime, deprivation, and drug use, were designated for redevelopment. Many tenants were re-housed—replaced by new modern office blocks and apartments. The offices included a building for the city council arts office, the Lab on the corner of Foley and James Joyce streets. These redevelopment plans stalled when the Celtic Tiger went bust leaving the remaining social housing Liberty House flats half lived-in and half boarded up, and the majority of retail units and offices left empty ("Liberty Corner," 2015) Louise Lowe, the director of Anu Productions, describes the company's fascination with these attempts to control this space saying:

> [i]t's an area when I look at it, its had four critical regenerations over a hundred years... its history within those regenerations has been really interesting to watch and to know why, why reinventing its streets or its name or its place or its position nothing very much has changed it's still an area that is quite dangerous to be around at nighttime or that you know has a sense of an undercurrent of never quite realising of who it is and what it is (interview, 2012).

The history of Foley Street is a history of the repeated failure of both colonial and national governments to establish ideological or behavioural control with formal architectural representational space. BOFS stages social interactions of an older street layout superimposed on a current architecture. Much of the production is inserted into hidden corners or forgotten left-over bits of the old architectures, like the last remaining flat in a partially boarded up and abandoned social housing complex. By performing oral history of past communities, the production highlights the lack of spatial practice of the current community, marginalized by a conceptual representation of space conceived of by urban planners.

The company consciously exploits the juxtaposition of performance and representations of space. Lowe calls the work, "a cubist dramaturgy in terms of pushing those two worlds together completely because I think what we're trying to do is to expose multiple surfaces simultaneously" (podcast, 2012). The choice of the word "expose" in the context of BOFS is interesting in terms of space. In the first two plays, you are exposing a distant social history of the Monto, and in *Laundry* [sic] the performance opened a forbidden building to expose it to the public. In BOFS, the spatial practice exposes or highlights the lack of communal and public space that is available in the latest regeneration. The result is that the performance is of characters whose lives are lived on the street and audiences are dragged into disused pockets of space off the main thoroughfare like a dead-end alley or the underside of a railway arch. These are places that the audience would not normally enter in terms of public safety. As one audience member explained about an interaction with a homeless character called Tommo:

> And he (Tommo) was quite intense he was commanding and demanding and just turning up the alley is unsettling because you know you are going into

areas that normally you wouldn't be in and you come to a dead end. You come to dead end and its "shit" there's this violent scene about to take place (Interviewee D).

An affective reaction to these challenging situations is an intensified awareness of the detail of place in this audient's perception. This is very possibly as a result of a "fight or flight" adrenaline reaction to the violence. The same audience member describes the visual impact when helping the beaten-up boy Git to look for his St. Christopher's medal in the alleyway:

> You know it's not the medal, you're noticing the little empty phials you know and there's dirty tracksuits and there's a bottle and bits of stuff that would probably be used for smoking or injecting or whatever and there's a few coins. So, you're actually noticing everything else that's on the ground (Interviewee D).

Ranciere's concepts concerning the emancipated spectator captivated by pensive images 'that existed solely in and through its relations either with other images or with texts' (108) seems to be supported by the audience reaction here (108). These images capture the ordinary subject, but as a result of framing it as art, the banality of the ubiquitous is destroyed and the everyday is rendered visible by art practice.

Once the potential of the pensive image is released, the performer can use this heightened engagement with subject matter to offer what Ranciere would refer to as an intolerable image where the stock reaction is "to close one's eyes or avert one's gaze" (85). In this case, the audience member is shown graphic pornography on a mobile phone. As the audience member is off kilter from the previous encounter, with the pensive image still struggling for causality and rational explanation, they initially watch to understand the pornography—though the instinctual response would normally be to turn away. This audience member is thrown into one of the first ethical dilemmas of collusion; with behaviour that would in everyday life be against their own natural instincts.

The sensory intensity of the experience deepens when the audience sit into a model of a 1970s car in the next installation scene. Here the haptic impact of low plastic leather seats combines with aural stimulation of seventies rock, radio news reports of the Talbot Street bombings, and a mutated stylized sound of a bomb explosion. This section has a slow durational aspect, as the performer, after an initial thump of a dead weight hitting the roof, slides in a slow motion across the roof and down the windshield of the car before standing and starting a monologue. This gives plenty of time to the audience member to absorb the deliberate historic layering of this space. For example, one audience member animatedly described:

> And then when you get down to the laneway I mean I was immediately bundled into the extremely bizarre car that my neighbour used to have in nineteen seventy-four or five that I remember sitting in the back of and all of a sudden this is a real flashback (Interviewee E).

Several audience members had a connection to the bombing event, whether it was merely a shared collective memory of trauma—for example one young woman too young to be alive at the time of the bombing shared a surname with one of the victims carved on the memorial stone opposite the train station (Interviewee H). But several people had more direct connections, disturbingly one audience member recalled:

> The car was very eerie because sitting in the car knowing that this body was on top! And it's strange because I worked when I was in college in the Educational Book Company schoolbook store just around the corner and I remember I worked on Saturday mornings and the bomb went off on the Friday. So, I went in to work as normal but it was just cleaning up the aftermath of it. So, it was kinda strange to be physically so close to where that had taken place and as if this girl had landed on top of the car (Interviewee D).

These are transmutations of collective memories into a social memory by the visceral reaction to the car space. Edward Casey, in his extensive research into phenomenological memory, has examined how social memory works in relation to commemoration. Social memory, he contends, requires a common place where history is enacted and experienced and that the history in that place is brought into communication with words or any other means of expression (Casey, 17–44). Here then, through the enactment of a place of memory, a co-reminiscence happens between the participant and the performer. So, the audience member is drawn into the social world of this place through this form of engagement with space as a memorial.

These collective memories and the audience members' access to that collective memory create what Ranciere would term a *sense* community with 'shared ways of perceiving, being affected and imparting meaning' (Ranciere, 103). This community are sharing not just sense data, but also modes of perception shaped by the design of the car installation and 'equally shareable meanings that are conferred on the data' (Ranciere, 102). For these reasons the scene is less coherent for a non-national audience member. For interviewee B, the car sequence was difficult to handle, as she had no contextual knowledge initially. In her own words:

> [t]he music's high and I'm a little anxious and I really feel like I don't know cos part of me as a conscientious audience participant I don't want to screw this up like am I supposed to talk to this woman am I supposed to help her like I wasn't sure what my level of participation was meant to be (Interviewee B).

This audience member has access to sharing ways of perceiving and being affected within this sense community, but without access to the collective memory, she lacks shared way of imparting meaning. Instead, the quotation highlights the audience focus on negotiating her experience in the car. In this way, she is moving beyond representations of Foley Street into a relationship with the space. This idea of here and now negotiation of space will be explored in the final section of the article in relation to Deborah Massey's understanding of place.

As the performance continues, the two audience members are reunited and driven across the area to the Liberty House flats. The second part of the performance is located in a domestic space and then a community meeting hall. It becomes apparent that what connects these disparate episodes is an interlinked path of overlapping and crisscrossing social actions. This is the last of Lefebvre's delineations of space. Here spatial practice creates a social space through the everyday life actions and behaviours propounded in the daily routine. Lefebvre refers to these practices as "urban reality (the routes and networks which link up the places set aside for work, private life and leisure)" (8). It is in this space that networks are generated "which are subordinated to the frameworks of politics" (Lefebvre, 117). In a sense, these discrete networks have broken down in BOFS. The audience experienced the public streets and lanes as the work place for drug pushers and dealers. These illegal behaviours are usually discreet and hidden from authority have colonized public space.

The private life of home and leisure in the flat scenes are corrupted as spaces of prostitution, violence, and danger. Inside one of the flats in the Liberty house complex, the audience has multiple encounters. In a tiny bathroom, big enough to house only a toilet and a wash hand basin facing it, a young woman character is dressing after being sexually abused. The main room contains a mother, schoolgirl, prostitute, and a young man spiraling out of control in a dysfunctional drink and drugs fueled party. Although different audience members experience different elements of these set-ups, they are all asked to engage in getting the abused young woman out of the house and finding her handbag. And in each experience, there is a moment of choreographed expressionism where the actors fling their bodies and each other around the room, in the case of the prostitute character, literally climbing the walls in wild physical manifestations of desperation and despair. It is during these sequences that the audience members are asked to dance and, in some cases, pulled into the whirling dervish of bodies in motion. It is a space of, at times, overwhelmingly intense energy for the audience. One participant described it as

> [t]he kind of enclosed space [that] was still really intimidating and you do really feel that people really living very physically on top of one another and therefore violence or sex is kinda just it's nearly unavoidable. It goes with the social deprivation but it also the intensity of living in someone else's space (Interviewee D).

But something else is evoked simultaneously in this spatial practice, what Bachelard in *The Poetics of Space* calls an oneiric home—one that we all carry with us and measure all other experiences of a home space against. Bachelard explores the intimate quality of a home as an internalized haptic knowledge of embodied experience. He describes this embodied knowledge as the house we were born into which "is physically inscribed in us. It is a group of organic habits" (Bachelard 14). The extreme distortions of home as a place of shelter in the flat provoke instinctual reactions from the audience rooted in this oneiric sense of home. One audience member generated, from her own actions in response to the bathroom girl scene, an unscripted improvised exchange in the kitchen area, described as follows:

I end up in the kitchen and I guess the mother with the broken nose she made a huge difference for me because…I complimented her on the smell because you are getting everything and I said 'that smells good' because you are in her KITCHEN and there's like this certain way that you are brought up you are in someone's house you are in their kitchen you should kind of respect her as a mother. We were in the kitchen; we were alone in the kitchen there was chaos out there but within this chaos it was a homey real place that was the only place in the whole thing that felt kind of comfortable (Interviewee B).

This oneiric home is a composite of dream and memory, an interpretation of the original actual place in which we assign imagined values to specific spaces. The audience member is establishing a social practice that is alien to the production but a part of a code of behaviour learnt and expounded in her version of the oneiric home to counteract the destructive energy that in her own words "almost made me break down" (Interviewee B). This kitchen performance encounter has generated a Lefebvrian social space constructed by the "outcome of a sequence and a set of operations" that "subsumes things produced, and encompasses their interrelationships in their coexistence and simultaneity" (73). It is such moments of unmediated improvised performativity generated in immersive audience practices that Nelson Barre is referring to in his article about the implicated audience of BOFS. He writes that the audience are "spectators [who] recognize and enact their own roles in this production and in the marginalizing culture of Ireland." Barre also contends that "these outsiders-made-participants can now recognize that the culturally constructed stories are not necessarily true." The remainder of this article demonstrates that this radical re-visioning is only possible if a fundamental shift happens for the audience in progressing their perception of Foley Street from a place to a practiced space. As the audience move towards the final scenes of the performance in the contemporary retail building (that is actually the Anu studio on James Joyce Street) the audience relationship to the area has potentially developed into a broader consciousness of place. Through immersing the audience in the physical properties and social practices of these spaces and opening up layers of memory, the audience have experienced a phenomenological engagement with a place as an inhabited space.

THE PLACE OF FOLEY STREET

This phenomenological encounter could, from a human geography perspective, be called a "place event." Doreen Massey created the concept of place event as a way of understanding place as a spatio-temporal event (2005, 130). Massey argues that what is special about a place is not in fact its essential pre-given absolute identity, but what she refers to as the…

Thrown togetherness, the unavoidable challenge of negotiating a here-and-now (itself drawing on a history and a geography of then and there); and a negotiation which must take place within and between both human and nonhuman (140).

In Massey's terms, we might call the performance mingling with the social world of Foley Street a situated process,

> ...woven together out of ongoing stories, as a moment within power geometries, as a particular constellation within the wider topographies of space, and as in process, an unfinished business (131).

The audience member who has entered the performance on listening to audio objectifying Foley Street and its inhabitants as a social problem and stood in a regenerated neighbourhood, ends up enmeshed in multiple power geometries. For example, in the bathroom scene, the spectator encounters a performer articulating a victim's experience of a real world act of sex in an imagined retelling of several newspaper archives from the victim's point of view. Told to look through holes in the wall at a screen with images playing that resolve into a snuff movie, a noise behind alerts the audience to the presence of another person in the small cubicle. The performer, semi-naked, starts to narrate her story in half-formed sentences. In the course of the broken monologue, the performer asks for help dressing and to fetch a handbag. She also asks the spectator's permission to leave at the end of the section.

The audience member is placed in a double position that their participative interactions may resolve. Initially a voyeur watching the snuff movie, next addressed as a person of power who can reclaim the victim character's belongings and release them. The rest of the rooms of the flat are dominated by the increasingly extreme physical and audio soundscape of the performer inhabitants of the flat. The bathroom is, for the spectator, a relatively calm haven and respite from sensory effects. However, the haptic and empathic exchange with the performer generates unease, disquiet and anger for audience members as the intimate exchange makes them feel a sense of responsibility and complicity in the abuse of the character.

The audience response to this type of spatial performance is acutely conscious of "power geometries." For Interviewee D, the intimacy of the bathroom and the audience member's presence in this space makes them an intruder. For her, it "was very unsettling because the privacy of the bathroom the privacy of watching the—she wipes herself you know and drops the rag. It's disturbing, upsetting and unsettling" (Interviewee D). For some, the process of place created a physical sensation.

> [t]hat bathroom with that awful wallpaper even what was going on it and the people that were in it and what was behind it that just it seems to be closing in on top of you. The locations suffocated as much as the people, the locations certainly made it intimidating as much as the people did (Interviewee F).

This is one example of how audiences at BOFS have negotiated their performance route in spatial practice with the performers. This generates another place event of this here and now, and the place event of performance becomes a further iteration of the identity of that location. In creating this visceral immersive experience for the audience, Anu offers a representational space for the audience that challenges the fearful avoidance of the area that had been these audience members relationship to representational space created by urban planning and negative media reports.

Conclusion

This article has taken a "thick description" approach to several audience members participative engagement and affective reactions to the immersive qualities of BOFS. This detailed analysis tracks a progressive development that is site responsive by these audience members as the level of complicity in the performance increases over the course of the performance event—as these participative actions are contextualized by the space the performance is operating in, as are the behaviours of the audience. This deepening engagement with a locale engages the audience member as a social actor. The lines are blurred between a performative and a place event. The distance required for an abstract representation of space is collapsed and the audience members have concluded the performance with potentially transfigured relationships to the streets and lanes they have briefly inhabited. One audience member described this as a revelatory experience:

> It's like the total unfamiliarity in a very familiar place. I drive down Gardiner St most weeks and two streets away there's in here…it's two streets away but it's a whole area I hadn't seen before. It was completely being totally at sea in a place that's really familiar. And that almost was kind of really disconcerting how do I not know about this, how am I so out of…this is my city (Interviewee E).

The power of Anu is that making the audience member complicit in a set of platial behaviours, highlights the total lack of choice and limits of social action for the character inhabitants. The audience descriptions of invasions of privacy, overwhelming claustrophobia, and physical intimidation are to paraphrase Massey moments of thrown togetherness in power geometries. The ultimate effect on the audience of the performance is that the powerlessness and disenfranchisement that allows a place like Foley Street, despite name changes and regenerations, to replicate itself across generations as a notorious space of deprivation, is temporarily a lived-experience for the audience. The audience leaving the area can now begin a new imaginative relationship with the abstracted space they [initially] approached with caution at the start of the performance.

Bibliography

Bachelard, Gaston, The Poetics of Space, Boston: Beacon Press, 1964. Boston.

Barre, Nelson. "'It's Crazy, That Was Us: The Implicated and Compliant Audience in The Boys of Foley Street." Comparative Drama 48.1–2 (2014): 103–16. Print.

Bennett, Susan, Theatre Audiences, Abingdon: Routledge, 1997.

Casey, Edward. "Public Memory in Place and Time." Public Memory, ed. Kendall Phillips Tuscaloosa: University of Alabama Press, 2004.17—44.

"Home|Dublin|Reflecting City." Liberty Corner. Web. 8 Aug. 2015.
http://www.reflectingcity.com/north-central/project-detail/liberty-corner/

Lanigan, Liam, James Joyce, Urban Planning and Irish Modernism: Dublins of the Future, Basingstoke: Palgrave Macmillan, 2014,

Lefebvre, Henri, Trans Nicholson-Smith, Donald, The Production of Space, Oxford: Blackwell, 1950.

Lowe Louise, "The Boys of Foley Street." Contemporary Irish Plays, ed. Lonergan, Patrick London: Bloomsbury, 2015. 347–400.

Lowe, Louise, Interview on Anu Productions: Process & Place. Interviewed by Pamela McQueen [in person] Anu Studio, Dublin. June 2012.

Lowe, Louise, "About Anu Productions" Web. Accessed 14 August 2014. http://anuproductions.wordpress.com/about/

Massey, Doreen, For Space, London: Sage, 2005.

Murphy, Sean J. "The Gardiner Family, Dublin, and Mountjoy, County Tyrone." Studies in Irish Genealogy and Heraldry Web. Accessed 14 August 2014. http://homepage.eircom.net/~seanjmurphy/studies/

Pierse, Michael. "The Miracle of Monto" Web. Accessed 8 August 2015. http://republican-news.org/archive/2002/September05/05mont.html

Interviewee B. Personal interview. 22 Sept. 2012.

Interviewee C. Personal interview. 22 Sept. 2012.

Interviewee D. Personal interview. 22 Sept. 2012.

Interviewee E. Personal interview. 22 Sept. 2012.

Interviewee H. Personal Interview. 29 Sept. 2012.

Ranciere, Jacques, The Emancipated Spectator, London: Verso, 2009.

"Rise Productions Irish Theatre Podcast." Interview. Audio blog post. I Tunes. Rise Productions, 30 May 2012. Web. 24 July 2014. https://itunes.apple.com/gb/podcast/rise-productions-irish-theatre/id479904411?mt=2

Singleton, Brian. "ANU Productions and Site-Specific Performance: The Politics of Space and Place." 'That Was Us': Contemporary Irish Theatre and Performance. Ed. Fintan Walsh. London: Oberon, 2013. Print.

CHAPTER 6

Re-Imagining Expectation for the Theatrical Event

Kendra Jones

EXPECTATION

Ask anyone their thoughts about the theatre, and their response will undoubtedly be steeped in nostalgia and expectation. Nostalgia for a particular experience or set of experiences remembered and no doubt somewhat extrapolated from some early encounter with the theatre, and highly steeped expectations based on this—that any new experience will be held to. There is an element of our minds which likes to revisit what is known, and in the best of cases, we learn something new from this new encounter with that story. Coupled with this, is the sense of how things ought to be. When it comes to theatre, in Western theatrical culture, we are ingrained from youth with practices and conventions; don't go on the stage, don't talk, watch the actors, get an ice cream at the interval, and applaud at the end. These expectations are the more outwardly acknowledged, the rules by which we agree to play. There are, however, less articulated expectations for what the theatrical event will bring; cultural betterment, making us a "better sort of person"—the "how" of this being nebulous, of course. Expectation, then, has the unlucky circumstance of being lumped in with this nostalgia. We, perhaps mistakenly, believe that audiences expect something familiar, both in terms of what they will see, and what the overall experience will be like. It is what we believe they want, and as a collective of theatre-makers (even if that feeling is somewhere deep down inside) we very often succumb to naturalistic, as-seen-on-TV style productions of stories that could just as easily, and perhaps more successfully, be told through another medium. Nostalgia is the easiest and most comfortable for artists to feed their audiences, as evidenced by the hundreds of productions of *A Christmas Carol* or countless musicals which look and sound the identical way that they did in their first production, or worse yet, their film adaptation. The expectation is that attending the theatre will "improve" us as audience members, and this is therefore seen as their inherent value. Any specifics are left out of the equation, and the fear of doing something new and different presides over productions. At the same time, we wonder why our audiences are dwindling, and continually struggle to justify the immense cost, both personal and monetary, of live performance. Why bother, when film is so prolific, when the quality of TV programs is so high, and everything is available at the click of a button without leaving your house. Predominantly, we appeal to nostalgia to fill this void, reminding audiences of the apparently inherent value in the form and the very act of attending the theatre, or of the personal benefit they will achieve, how they will feel better about themselves for learning something. We sit in this stagnation, rather than risk, and this self-fulfilling circle is toxic and unfruitful. Certainly, we have a responsibility to ourselves and our audiences to do more.

Let us consider some of the relatively recent major shifts in the English-speaking theatre; absurdism, including Beckett and Ionesco, which shocked us by devaluing language and personal relationships. John Osborne and the Angry Young Men who unsettled us by putting a kitchen sink and working class accents on stage. Sarah Kane who aggressively confronted us with the ugly realities of our modern world. The deconstructionist approach centralized authorship, bringing us the collective creation which further reformed our relationship with the theatre-making authorship no longer the act of a single individual. These few examples, and countless others, have one common thread; that they sought to shake-up form as it was known, taking away what was familiar to drive us to pay closer attention. Contemporary practitioners have begun in the past ten or so years to add their voice to the newest shift; that of the immersive. Borrowing ideas about the audience relationship from Artaud to Genet, from performance artists to musicians, and from observation of real life experiences, we have begun to create this new form. Coupled with what Hans-Thies Lehmann has called the Post-Dramatic, the immersive embraces our non-linear post-post-modernist socially digitized and audibly fragmented experience, and creates a theatre that urgently speaks to the audience once again, through the denial of the familiar and the comfortable. Denial, ultimately, of those core conventions of the theatre we are taught to follow as children; placement of the audience in the midst of the action, taking them from their comfortable chair with a distance from the actors to the centre of the event. At its core, this new work stems from a heightened awareness of the audience, their relationship with the work they are seeing in the moment, and the expectations they brought to the theatre with them. This formal shift is not simply a flash in this moment, but rather a necessary piece of the evolutionary ecosystem of the theatrical landscape to ensure the continuance of the art form.

This work takes on many forms; however at its core, the focus is on the relationship with the audience. This is an investigation some of the variety of forms of the immersive, and the core methods for engaging the audience relationship in the work of my company, impel theatre. Impel is that which drives or urges forward; which challenges and imparts motion to [sic]. I hope that through reading this chapter, you will be incited to impel your own work to a more thorough and thoughtful understanding of its relationship with the audience and their expectations.

THE STATE OF THEATRE

One of the ways I like to begin work with a group of actors, whether student or professional, is to ask them a few brief questions; what is your favourite thing you've seen in the theatre, and why? What was your worst experience as an audience member, and why? Normally, I get responses about seeing a ballet or a holiday production of some kind that cemented this person into wanting a class or two, or perhaps a life in the theatre; and the negative most commonly associates itself to an audience member not following the rules in some way—a person fell asleep, cell phone rang, people walking out, all kinds of perceived misbehaviours. These responses, note, are all steeped in expectation! This is good; it provides us a starting point and enables us to look at how to make the kind of theatre we think is interesting, rather than simply what we think is popular or profitable. One of my own earliest memories of the theatre is of seeing a wonderfully playful and engaging production at Winnipeg's Prairie Theatre Exchange of *The Snow Queen* when I was quite small; my (now foggy) memory is one of a piece of theatre that was playful, and full of magic—luring me to feel as though I was inside the story myself. Every subsequent production I saw there and elsewhere paled in comparison. For years, I did not experience another show that held this same magic over me. I saw countless productions, seeking the experience of feeling the show was *just for me,* and despite seeing good performances, they always felt vacant. Somewhere in the back of my mind, my own ideas about audience relationship to the work, and the seed of the idea of immersive work, was born. I began to question (and wonder) how you could take an audience of hundreds, and make them feel engaged as individuals, not simply as part of a group.

Recently, I was confronted with a student who clearly was brought to the theatre class under duress, and when I asked my usual starter questions, he stated quite boldly (and I suspect expecting a certain kind of response) that he hated theatre, and hadn't ever seen anything he liked. I warmed to the student immediately, and shared with the whole group, that if I was perfectly honest, I didn't like most theatre either. The whole reason I began making theatre was because I felt dissatisfied with what I was seeing and what was available to me. To be frank, it was often boring; aimed itself at goals when it's most simple and important task, of keeping my attention, was not met. The theatre I saw never quite felt like it had something to say, or if it did, it was never sufficiently successful at making me aware of that thing. Martin Esslin put it quite clearly;

> "Put in its simplest and most mundane terms, the basic task of anyone concerned with presenting any kind of drama to any audience consists in capturing their attention and holding it as long as required. Only when that fundamental objective has been achieved can the more lofty and ambitious intentions be fulfilled; the imparting of wisdom and insight, poetry and beauty, amusement and relaxation, illumination and purging of emotion. If you lose their attention, if you fail to make them concentrate on what is happening, on what is being said, all is lost."[1]

So, I have set out in my own work, and have observed in this new immersive work in pockets around the world, a desire to grab and hold on to the audience's attention using traditional means but as never seen before. Certainly, just having people on stage talking is not going to be sufficient any longer. As visionary director Julie Taymor states, "We end up using very little of our brains and imaginations if we just

---

[1] Esslin, Page 43.

stick to people talking."[2] We need to capture imaginations, to create new worlds where the audience is engaged physically and intellectually, and ultimately they are complicit in the theatrical event, not simply sitting back and observing. We are presented, then, with the predicament of how to do this. How can we create a space where it is possible for audiences to engage in this way?

First, and foremost, we must challenge the sanctity of the theatrical space. The space for theatre—traditional and dedicated theatre buildings, with proscenium arches or even in the round, where audiences sit in the dark and observe—is an enemy to this new audience engagement. These buildings are intimidating to those who have not attended a show in them before; they can be imposing and impersonal, filled with things that are intimidatingly intellectual and not easily understood. These buildings are unfamiliar; and rather than serve as a central focal point of a community, are a refined refuge for a small and elite group. This relationship to many of the theatre buildings in our communities is at odds with the stories and truths that make up theatre now. "Theatre is a far broader church now—and a less sacred one, less sanctimonious" as Tim Bano argued, "It's [sic] a stunning ecology, imperfect and unequal, but always wanting to make things better, always responding to and trying to remedy the present and the past."[3] It is our responsibility to spread the word of this change.

In his *Phenomenology of the Theatre*, Bert States argues that, "the history of theatre can be viewed as a history of flirtation with the physical distance between stage and audience"[4] and it is in this very distance that the opportunity for audience engagement lies. We have emerged from a period of intense distancing, both in the sense of Brechtian *verfremmdungseffekt*, and in the more naturalist sense of traditional proscenium distance between actors and audience; and [now] embark upon a period of immersion, where the distance is blurred, obscured, and at times even eliminated entirely. In these immersive performances, the performer and the audience both have an experience of connection with another human (the audience and performer each having an effect on the other), and emerging [sic] with a cognizance of this affect [sic] and interrelation of our collective set of human experiences. The performer is not simply a vessel, but a conspirator who is experiencing and molding the world around them at the same time as their auditor. This is immersion. Within this encounter, there is a sense of responsibility for the experience of the audience held by the performers, ensuring that the audience feel safe and able to release their expectations. It differs from conventions of audience participation, in which audience members are called up on stage to perform a rather typically embarrassing task for the enjoyment of the other audience members—a laugh begotten at their good humoured expense. This sort of interaction, too, plays on expectation—the expectation that the unprepared and untrained audience member will behave in a way to elicit a laugh. The audience in the immersive, however, is positioned with a responsibility to the world in which they find themselves. Their interaction can be physical, or intellectual, but it is always for the mutual benefit of themselves and the performers, rather than for the amusement of

---

[2] Taymor
[3] Bano
[4] States, Page 96

80

the larger group at their expense. In this space, expectation becomes the medium, to borrow from Marshall McLuhan. The theatre-maker sets up a space which seems like one thing, using expectation to create a sense of comfort and familiarity, and then subverts these expectations to unsettle the auditor, and draw attention to something specific in this experience, heightening the audience member's attentiveness. I recently listened to Dominic Cooke discussing work on a new play with the National Theatre[5], and he echoed this desire to unsettle the audience, simply to increase their attention to what is placed in front of them. The theatre space is one where it is easy to have information and beauty wash over you from a distance, where even the most chilling or unsettling stories can feel separated from your own experience; I recall seeing a performance of Edward Bond's *Saved* at the Lyric Hammersmith in 2011, in a theatre filled with large groups of students in their teens. The baby stoning scene, which had been spine chilling to me when reading the play years before, lost some of its intensity, and the audience picked up on this. Rather than the stunned silence one would expect at seeing this act on stage, many of the young students laughed. This was not the uncomfortable laugh of a teenager who sees something that they don't know how to deal with, but rather the laugh of someone recognizing the falsity of what was in front of them. This is a particular challenge—to ensure these terrible moments in a play are felt for their gravitas, and an opportunity for theatre-makers to look for ways to ensure this moment hits home.

I should note that this unsettling may sound rather aggressive in its description, however it need not be. The differences can be subtle; a simple uneasiness, or sense that something is "off," may be sufficient to set the audience's attention on alert, and therefore result in their incrusted attentiveness to the form and content of the theatrical work. That said, there are occasions where a more aggressive form of unsettling may be suitable. This is, of course, at the discretion of the creator, at the bidding of the needs of the play, and perhaps most importantly, beholden to the experience of the audience.

While the architecture of the space and the overall feeling of the experience are fundamental to the immersive, the actual experience of the immersion is personal— this is theatre which can speak to individuals collectively, rather than as a part of a collective. This can be Punchdrunk[6] transforming hotels or warehouses and letting you to feel you are in charge of your own path through the performance; or a space that is constricted in some ways, but causes a visceral and personal reaction with heightened awareness. It can be immersing a person in an unfamiliar space and set of experiences in the way of *You Me Bum Bum Train*[7], or simply calling attention to things you see and do every day, in the way of Rosana Cade's *Walking:Holding*[8] and *How We Met*[9] by Eleanor Massie and Holly Bragg. But what is common among these practices is their undeniable focus on the individual audience member's experience and intellectual engagement with the space and ideas. In some practices (such as Run

---

[5] Cooke

[6] In particular, Sleep No More and Faust among their productions. More at *http://punchdrunk.com*

[7] For more on Run Riot's You Me Bum Bum Train visit *http://www. bumbumtrain.com*

[8] For more info visit *https://rosanacadedotcom.wordpress.com/ projects/walkingholding/*

[9] RADA Festival, London. July 2012.

Riot or Punchdrunk), the lead performer is the audience member, and the actors are simply there to create an environment. In such practices, the audience is positioned as the discoverer or creator of the story; the actors are there to support this discovery, turning the traditional role of the audience as auditor (or viewer) on its head. Even in the seemingly traditionally structured practices of companies such as Schaubühne Berlin (in terms of quite often performing in physical theatres with prosceniums), this distance is challenged, and audience members are run past, their images taken on video projected to the stage, or engaged in a loud and shouted debate about ethics in society. This feels necessary in a world of distancing, where digital devices separate us even when we sit next to one another—immersion is a means to truly engage and awaken our audiences, and the method takes many shapes. To make them feel out of sorts and therefore highly aware, and ultimately more susceptible to the message and intent of the piece, on an unconscious, pre-verbal level.

FORMATIVE EXPERIENCES

My own encounters with the current forms of immersive theatre came through exposure to many of these very productions. I was a performer in a 2011/2012 edition of *You Me Bum Bum Train (YMBBT)*, playing multiple roles in various different parts of the experience. At the time, I knew little of what immersive theatre meant, and held some of the expectations lingering from experiences of terrifying audience participation. And yet, I was drawn to the concept, and volunteered. The experience was eye-opening, and I noted my observations in blog posts during the performance period, observing,

> "[t]his specific production gives such ultimate care to the emotional ride of the passenger—in fact they call the performance a ride—each scene, and the succession of them, is carefully crafted to take a person through the highs and lows of human experience, but with a sense of safety that allows them to play."[10]

Each night, we would bring through a number of passengers, and experience their joys, fears, and apprehensions at each new experience they were immersed in [sic]. Rather than the typical setup where it is the actors who play on the stage, this production (and those like it) provide the audience the opportunity to play, in a manner that hearkens back to childhood imagination games. *YMBBT* is unique among immersive theatrical events, as it does not just create a single experience, but a chain of micro experiences, giving the passenger an array of events outside their every day that they most likely would never have the opportunity to experience. What was most distinct was the observation that each passenger experienced the spaces differently; within the same space, one passenger would react with joy, another with unbridled giggling and nerves, another with frozen apprehension, and so on. Coupled with this, our experience as performers morphed; in performing, each night I would come home

---

[10] Jones, Kendra. Reflections-The Audience.

feeling as though I, too, had gone on a journey. Not one of a variety of spaces, however, but one of a variety of human experiences and reactions to a single particular event—one that was distinctly theatrical, but also notably not dramatic. The simultaneous similarity, and uniqueness of each of the human beings who passed through was apparent. The distinct characteristics of each passenger's experience was apparent to the performers, and shaped our experience of the repetitive task of creating the same scene 15 or 20 times per night. The sensation of a passenger really playing along, compared with the struggle to keep the scene going when a passenger was resistant or unusually quiet, contrasted, and we experienced the extremes along with the range between [sic]. Unlike previous performance experiences where the actors have a sense of the audience as a collective, with this sort of immersive performance, the actors gain a knowledge of the audience as individual and autonomous beings, and their unique responses. The productions are shrouded in secrecy; details of the ride are kept secret, and no photos are shared. Those who have been through the show are asked to keep their experiences to themselves and not share in detail, particularly on social media. The personal nature of these experiences is paramount, and the impact of this hinges on expectation—or to be more clear, a lack thereof. Passengers expect only a surprise. They are unable to build up an intellectual preparation, and therefore are confronted with the situations and respond organically in the moment of experience.

Thomas Ostermeier's *Hamlet* for Schaubühne Berlin[11] was a more traditionally constructed theatrical experience upon initial view; however, it positioned us in the audience as accomplices in a way I had not previously experienced. Lars Eidinger played the Danish prince—fat, constantly eating and drinking, petulant—running through the audience, speaking to us directly, and shoving his video camera (which projected to a massive screen upstage) in our faces. The production's frantic energy was extended to us; we, too, felt as though we were teetering on the edge of witnessing a disaster, yet utterly helpless to act against it. In fact, the performance I witnessed was one in which that line between planned theatrical playfulness and real injury crossed, when Eidinger hit his head on the cement of the lodges; although frightening in retrospect, in the moment, because the production had been so successful in pulling us along in this man's frenzy, it wasn't clear whether that, too, wasn't just another staged pratfall to make us aware of our inability to do anything. In an instance such as this, expectation played a different role, but was pivotal nonetheless. Ostermeier's work is preceded by its reputation; the promotion for the show indicated a 3 hour *Hamlet*, in German. Thus one prepares for something that may be intellectually challenging (particularly to non-German speakers); it is this preparation that enables the surprise of a visceral and quite literally [sic] dirty performance in a mud pit, where language takes its shape in the body and images just as much (if not perhaps more so than from the voice).

The third formative experience in my experimentations with the immersive came in the form of a new short work called *How We Met*[12] by Holly Bragg and Eleanor Massie, which I supported the workshop of and eventual performance in the inaugural

---

[11] Shakespeare, William. Hamlet. Dir. Thomas Ostermeier.

[12] Massie, Eleanor and Bragg, Holly. How We Met. Dir. Eleanor Massie and Holly Bragg.

RADA Festival in Bloomsbury, London. A promenade performance accompanied by audio play, this piece delved into the experience of walking through a busy London street in midday. Audience members experienced the piece one-on-one; meeting in RADA's bar on Gower street, they were given instructions to sit at a specific table, put on the provided headphones and press play. Then, to follow the girl with the blue backpack. From there, the audience member was taken on a walk through Bloomsbury, where actors were placed in a choreographed manner; the performers would appear and reappear in different places that the audience member was guided to, and would perform everyday tasks such as applying lip gloss or reading the newspaper in a specific choreography, sometimes solo and sometimes in perfect synchronicity with one another. The audience was invited to take note of the individuals they observed, and the particularity with which individuals take up personal tasks in a public place. In this particular performance, the act of waiting was a notable part of the experience both for the audience member—who waited in anticipation of their guide—and for the performers, who waited in a public place, and repeated tasks. The feeling was an unusual combination of the utter privacy involved in any acting performance, and a feeling of consistently being watched, even in the "off" moments where the intended audience was not present. The necessity of waiting, and of solitude, resulted in yet another commonality between performer and audience experience. I noted during the performance period:

> "As a performer in this kind of piece, with your small but important pattern to perform repeatedly, feelings of loneliness and solitude are evoked. Much like the people enjoying the performance, the performers are simultaneously together (as a unit) but alone (doing their specific sequence). Not unlike people every day in life, who are together in this experience of London in July of 2012, but alone in our own path and perspective. The performer experience thus reflects the audience experience, taking the performer on a journey as well."[13]

Our performance space was visible to the paying audience, but also like Boal's Invisible Theatre, to all others around, as they undoubtedly took note of the behaviours and repetition as well. In one notable experience, the lines between performer and the "set" of the real world grew particularly blurred, as a non-performer ate her lunch in the park, and the audience member paused to observe her actions as well. Thus, the desired effect of procuring genuine interest in seeing and understanding those around us was heightened further than we could have imagined. Expectation was at play once again here; the audience expects that all things placed in front of them are for their consumption and enjoyment, and derive meaning from even the most insignificant or unintentional.

These particular experiences and the observations relating to them led me to a greater desire to deconstruct the understanding of our relationship with the audience, and our relationship with the works of art themselves, as well as the role expectation (or lack of expectation) can play in the impact of the theatrical event. The theatricality

---

[13] Jones, Kendra. The Performer Experience.

84

inherent in the everyday was increasingly apparent to me as the building blocks for these experiments in the immersive, and led me to creative experiments described below.

IMPEL THEATRE: AUTEL[14]

Autel was the first of my own immersive installation projects. It began with a criticism; I was finding myself frustrated with the intellectual distance that I was observing audiences placing between themselves and art, regardless of the form. I had been spending considerable time in art galleries, both classical and contemporary, overhearing conversations about the work. Observing people's physical stance in relationship to the painting or sculpture, or listening to their postured conversations at the interval. The goal of *Autel* was to make audiences aware; first of themselves and their own vanity, and subsequently of the vanity of those around them taking in other works of art. Audience members were invited to sit one at a time in front of a mirror at a dressing table adorned with lipstick, mirrors, lace, and an iPod with headphones with which there was an instruction to "press play." The iPod held a short audio play, comprised like a found poem from text written by Jean Genet and Antonin Artaud, performed by me. It was structured in two waves; first, the audience member was welcomed in, flattered, cajoled, and comforted. The tone then quickly switched to one of criticism for this vanity, calling out the audience member's self-aggrandizement. Following this, it invited the audience member to be complicit in the act of judging this same vice in the others in the gallery space; looking in the mirror at those behind them (who were observing other works of art), the play called out the inauthentic nature of the gallery experience of art, which imposes knowledge and meaning which perhaps may not be intended (or in fact, there at all).

Observing audience members in both the showing at the Royal Academy of Dramatic Art, and at the Gas Station Arts Centre, it was highly informative to watch the audience members as they experienced the piece. The cycle of emotions was clearly visible, as audience members relaxed back while flattered, leaned in to the mirror as the flattery grew, and then froze when criticized, relaxing upon the feelings of complicity in the observance of the vice in others around them.

IMPEL THEATRE: *DEAR MAMA*[15]

This led to further desire to take control over audience reactions to the work. Complicity continued to be a theme in the work as I went in to developing *Dear Mama*. On its surface, *Dear Mama* is a traditional play; it is performed in a theatre, by an actor, and tells a story. That said, the structure of the story, and the physical creation of the space is what makes it a sort of immersion. The theatre space used in the initial production was a studio in an upper floor of a heritage building. Upon entry to the theatre space, there were tables, lamps, and decorations to make the audience

---

[14] Jones, Kendra. Autel.
[15] Jones, Kendra. Dear Mama.

feel as though they had entered someone's house. All lighting during the performance was done via these regular household lamps, with no traditional stage lighting. As they play opens, Ruby is in her 60s and comes out chatting to the crowd, telling jokes, thanking them for coming—as if a star in a Vegas-style celebrity show. What ensues is a stream-of-consciousness performance as the character transforms between herself at sixty-five, at eighteen, and at six. The audience see sexualized behaviours in the older women, the crisis of identity this causes, and the training of these sexualized and objectified behaviours in the youngest character, who is actively looking to please. While the youngest two of the characters have no "outside" character that we hear, the oldest, Ruby, has an "audience" manifested by a laugh track. Early in the play, this serves to make the audience comfortable and relaxed, so that when they begin to see the behaviours that are recognizable in that sort of older faded performer, they laugh (as we all so often do). However, as these images begin to juxtapose with the images of the tortured 18 year-old, and the eager to please 6 year-old, the audience is positioned to be highly aware of and attentive to their complicity in the creation of these occurrences in everyday life. As the play continues, the laugh track appears less and less, until it disappears completely, confronting the audience with their own laughter, and the sadness of this individual whose self-worth is defined entirely by others' perception of her.

Each performance of *Dear Mama* was followed by a talkback, in which I sought out the audience's questions and feelings on the piece. Every night an overwhelming number of audience members indicated that as they watched, they felt as though they needed to do something about what they were seeing, to try to stop what was happening to the young girl, but constrained by the understanding of appropriate audience behaviour in a theatre (and of course, the knowledge that it was a play, and the performer wasn't really six years old). This was most exciting; to have the ability to elicit such a visceral response from the audience within and perhaps as a result of using the constraints of traditional theatre etiquette to our benefit was highly rewarding. And most importantly, audience members commented that although it was difficult, they loved and appreciated the feeling of complicity and that need to act on what they were seeing.

This worked in similar ways to *Autel,* however this time the individual feelings were experienced as a group; a unique opportunity to bring people together to feel the same thing in a non-confrontational manner.

IMPEL THEATRE: THE FIRST TIME[16]

I began to think on the theatricality of things we do every day. As we go out in public, we perform certain persona depending on the place we are visiting, the reason for us being there, and our relationship with the place. There are certain expectations we have, and that are had of us. We also have expectations as to what theatre is (typically: in a room, with a story) and who it is for (people in theatres, the "it's not for me" argument from young people). Through the codification of theatrical spaces,

---

[16] Jones, Kendra. The First Time.

we have made them somewhat unapproachable for those who do not feel they know the rules, or who feel that the work is boring. So, I set out to create a piece of theatre which broke all these rules, in fact not even describing itself as a theatrical experience, but rather as an audio journey. *The First Time* was born of these thoughts. An audio play, it was written by me based on observations of people attending music events, and specifically music festivals. Here too, there is a codification of behaviour, and also a space that to some may feel foreign and uninviting. So, *The First Time* was a guided tour of this space, aimed at bringing both views together. Audience members could download the audio play to their headphones, and meet at an assigned location at a specified time. They began the audio at the assigned time, and then followed a performer as instructed, who guided them on a walk toward a music performance. The piece took place at the Manitoba Electronic Music Exhibition of Technology, Innovation and Creativity (MEME Festival) in Winnipeg, which showcases digital performance, and the assigned time was to conflate with the live DJ performance of John Norman.

The piece was, in some ways, my biggest experiment to date. Completely outside the context of formal art and theatre, the audio play existed as a supplement to a live DJ set. Two very interesting things occurred. First, although the observations about the behaviours of people in the audio recording were truthful, there were no actors positioned to correspond with them; so the audio may have asked the audience member to look to the right of the stage, or at a group of people dancing in a particular way, however there was no guarantee this would actually be happening. Something very interesting occurred, however, wherein random individuals in the crowd at the festival who were not listening to the audio play began to behave in the ways that were being discussed. The second thing is that those listening to the audio play were wearing headphones; an uncanny number of people came up to them as I observed, asking them what they were doing—several downloaded the play and listened to the experience on their own later on as well. This was a particularly successful experiment in seeing whether expectations can be subverted, and also in discovering what happens when so many elements are left up to chance in a creative experiment such as this.

IMPEL THEATRE: TONIGHT AT EIGHT[17]

This piece was born of an observation upon reading many plays by Noël Coward—that the true aspect of fun in his plays exists in the parties that occur on stage. Thus, for the Royal Manitoba Theatre Centre's Master Playwright Festival, rather than present a Coward play, my creative partner Stephanie Plaitin of Selardi Theatre and I provided an opportunity for audience members to experience a Coward play. The event took place in the RAW Gallery in Winnipeg, and was promoted with a rather coy and playful message to simply "expect the unexpected." Despite telling very little of what the play would entail, other than it was a special experience and available for one night only, the event sold out! Expectation and anticipation can go hand in hand.

---

[17] Jones, Kendra and Plaitin, Stephanie. Tonight at Eight.

The play itself took place around the gallery, with four lead actors whose characters were improvised loosely based on characters found in minor Coward one-act plays. The actors were provided [sic] their character outline, and we created an overall arc of the event, and provided four "staff"—these took the form of volunteers who were "in" on the piece, and knew what was going to happen, to help direct the audience's attention. From there, we let things run loose. The audience was welcomed in to the gallery space and immediately greeted by one of the staff posing as a maid, who processed their tickets and provided them with game tokens, then rang for the hosts. Each individual was brought in to the space and shown around by one of the two primary actors, as if they were an old friend, and encouraged to have fun. Plot points were loosely dropped to the audience members, but not with consistency, so that each person or group had a slightly different bit of information. As the room filled, additional actors arrived, and the relationships between the four primary actors spread around the room, with the audience taking space, and participating in games on their own and with the actors. Thus, the forty-five minute show proceeded; audience members heard pieces of arguments or gossip, listened to music, played games, and occasionally watched the actors do things. It culminated in a staged fight between two of the actors, and one storming out, which was a focal point regardless of where the audience was situated. What was notable was that our expectations—that the audience would just sit and watch—were incorrect! The audience dove in so wholeheartedly to the games and party provided to them, that the volunteer staff actually had to help direct attention more than we had anticipated. In fact, the participation was the opposite of what we had anticipated, thinking that the audience would be shy in this sort of environment.

Upon reflection, and in speaking with members of the audience afterward, they described the experience as one truly unique; they had seen things, and compared information and observations with the other audience members, and in many cases just had a plain good time. One audience member described it as, "a confused transcendence," which if I may try to unpack, I believe is an indication of the transcendence of expectations. The audience *were* the play, rather than spectators of the play, and they found it delightful!

IMPEL THEATRE: POPART INSTALLATIONS[18]

The pop ART series of installation pieces are creations wherein I aim to bring an experience of the theatrical nature of our relationship with particular spaces, and heighten our awareness of how we experience and interact with the unknown. Perhaps the most experimental of the works listed so far, the pop ART series, are the furthest from the typical definition of theatre. There is no script, and there are no actors. A space is selected for a certain feeling it evokes, and I subsequently bring on a musician and a video artist to help create a specific experience of that space.

Project Vapour was the first such experiment. Situated in a long and dark alley, the experience was created in midafternoon, tucked away beside a busy street during

---

[18] Jones, Kendra. pop ART. Series.

the Winnipeg Fringe Theatre Festival. The alley was blocked off from one end, and the musician, along with a structure for projection, were placed at this blocked off end, with a rather loud sound system. Music was played, and the projections done in the structure; however, from afar, these things looked highly unusual. Music and visual effects typically reserved for a nightclub or warehouse party were there in the middle of the day. As people walked past the alley, they would pause in wonder at what was going on. Without encouragement, they would slowly walk up the alley toward the music, exploring their curiosity about what was happening. As they did so, their experience became less like a bright and sunny Sunday afternoon, and more like a dark night time party. Some chose to stand and watch, others explored the projection structure and images, while still others began dancing for a time. After a time, people would then leave, although we noted that many would return back, pausing at the entrance and often coming back in to the space, bringing friends. It is precisely this sense of curiosity, of experiencing something that did not seem to belong in that space and time which was the goal of the piece–positioning audience members in a way that piqued their interest, and challenging them in a friendly way to try something new.

Intersection had a slightly different focus. Taking place on Nuit Blanche, where experimentation and unusual art experiences are already what people expect, this piece was created with the goal of drawing attention to the ways in which different artistic practices can support and enhance one another. Our piece began with a space: The Royal Winnipeg Ballet's outdoor atrium, which is angular and harsh, but still has a welcoming feeling to it. Here, we situated musician Ali Khan with a small amount of musical studio gear creating loops and songs live, and paired him with mapped projections from jaymez. The projections mapped the many lines and angles on the building, and the photograph of two principal RWB Dancers that was on the wall. The projections were live mixed, causing the space to move and morph, making the dancers look like they were moving at times, and all in tandem with the live music. Additionally, we had some fantastic happenstance, wherein dancers, cyclists, fire dancers, and hula hoop dancers (to name a few) took over the open ground in front of the projections to dance. These intersections of the work, demonstrating how the practices complemented on another, were astounding. Many audience members stood mesmerized at the multiple forms of creative work occurring in front of their eyes. The liveness of the performances, and improvisational nature of their individual work and their relationships to one another was captivating.

RE-IMAGINING EXPECTATION

These observations bring us to a new conclusion. Whereas previous shifts in the English-speaking theatre were highly intellectual in their form, and at times alienating to audiences, the immersive uses alienation as a tool to engage the audiences in a visceral experience which triggers the intellectual, but is not crafted around it. In a creative space where digital media is central, and it is increasingly simple for individuals to be the focal point to a narcissistic level, the immersive offers an opportunity to use these limitations, rather than have to work against them. There have been events in the past year where audiences are outraged when less experienced audience members behave in what is deemed an inappropriate manner, such as the cell phone incident on Broadway, or the ringing phone at the Barbican. However, these outrages, while understandable as a manifestation of the frustration at a perceived disrespect for the performers, are actually an opportunity. If we as theatre-makers make it our responsibility to understand the expectations inherent in the theatrical space, and the codification of these behaviours, and use these as tools to engage those who do not know and heighten the experience of the work, we have a unique opportunity to engage new audiences rather than to alienate them. This work hinges on the unknown, and our inherent curiosity. The level of the unknown and the ability to discover something new and unique titivates us in a world of the hyper-informed and the hyper-reported. There are so few surprises, and such distance in our interpersonal interactions which take place so heavily over digital mediums that the person-to-person connection with someone you do not know in the performer/audience relationship is truly surprising and unique. This work requires a constant awareness that we are watching something that is a work of art, and not something that is real, therefore requiring that we have a perspective on it. This byproduct is perhaps the most valuable of all in the benefits of the immersive; popular culture makes everything we encounter hyper-real, and thus it can be a challenge to distinguish. This essence of the real, but with a necessity of a critical position, brings the audience member a heightened awareness of not only the theatrical experience, but a heightened awareness they may carry into the every day.

There will always be a place for the traditional work, however its place grows smaller as new forms present themselves and become a part of the milieu. The work of artists such as Tim Crouch blurs these lines, making script based traditional location theatre in a way that challenges the audience's conception of their role. Companies like Punchdrunk push us far outside of the regularly accepted realm. And there is a whole range of experiences between; where my own work here lies, and where there is ample opportunity to experiment with these expectations, and the overall audience relationship to create something truly unique. And truly necessary.

WORKS CITED

Bano, Tim. *The Knight from Nowhere/The Bells: On Henry Irving, the history of acting and museum-piece theatre.* Exeunt Magazine, London. Accessed 5 December, 2015. http://exeuntmagazine.com/reviews/knight-from-nowhere-the-bells/

Cooke, Dominic. *National Theatre Platforms: Dominic Cooke on Here We Go.* Accessed Jan 4, 2016. http://www.nationaltheatre.org.uk/discover/platforms/dominic-cooke-on-here-we-go

Esslin, Martin. *An Anatomy of the Theatre.* Farrar, Straus and Giroux, 1977. Page 43. Print.

Jones, Kendra. *Autel.* Written & created by Kendra Jones, 2012 based on text from Jean Genet and Antonin Artaud. Performed at the Royal Academy of Dramatic Art (London, UK July 2012) and The Gas Station Arts Centre (Winnipeg, Canada October 2012). Performance Installation.

Jones, Kendra. *Dear Mama.* Written & performed by Kendra Jones. Directed by Megan Andres, produced by impel theatre for RMTC Master Playwright Festival: SondheimFest 2013, at Studio Incarnate, Winnipeg, Canada (February 2013). Live Performance.

Jones, Kendra. *The First Time.* Written by Kendra Jones, performed by Pamela Roz and John Norman for MEME Festival 2013 at Old Market Square in Winnipeg, Canada.

Jones, Kendra. *The Performer Experience.* Blog post July 4, 2012. http://impeltheatre.blogspot.ca/2012/07/performer-experience.html

Jones, Kendra. *pop:ART Series.* pop ART: Project Vapour was performed July 19, 2015 during the Winnipeg Fringe Festival at Artspace. Created & Curated by Kendra Jones, audio by John Norman, visual by Pixel Pusher. Live Performance.

Jones, Kendra. *pop:ART Series.* popART: Intersection was performed September 29, 2015 as an official selection for Nuit Blanche Winnipeg. Created & Curated by Kendra Jones, audio by Ali Khan, visual by jaymez.Live Performance.

Jones, Kendra. *Reflections-The Audience.* Blog post, December 21, 2011. http://impeltheatre.blogspot.ca/2011/12/reflectioins-audience.html

Jones, Kendra & Plaitin, Stephanie. *Tonight at Eight.* Conceived, created, and directed by Kendra Jones and Stephanie Plaitin, performed by Rodrigo

Beilfuss, Daina Leitold, Karl Thordarson, and David Jacob at RAW Gallery in Winnipeg. Produced by impel theatre and selardi productions. (February 2015). Live Performance.

Massie, Eleanor & Bragg, Holly. *How We Met* . Dir. Eleanor Massie and Holly Bragg. RADA Festival, London. July 2012. Live Performance.

Shakespeare, William. *Hamlet*. Dir. Thomas Ostermeier. Produced by Schaubuhne Berlin, performed at The Barbican, London. December 2011. Live Performance.

States, Bert O. *Great Reckoning In Little Rooms: On the Phenomenology of Theatre.* University of California Press. Los Angeles and Berkeley. 1985. Page 96. Print.

Taymor, Julie. "Julie Taymor on the Art of Spectacle in Theatre" interviewed by Shad. *The Q.* Canadian Broadcasting Corporation. Aired Dec 10, 2015. http://www.cbc.ca/radio/q/schedule-for-thursday-december-10-2015-1.3358643/julie-taymor-on-the-art-of-spectacle-in-theatre-1.3358649

CHAPTER 7

Art, Pedagogy, and Innovation: Tracing the Roots of Immersive Theatre and Practive

Pamela Sterling and Mary McAvoy

"I wanted to create productions where the audience is physically present, so that they are driven by a base, gut feeling and making instinctive decisions. That sort of show leaves a far larger imprint on you than just watching something."

—Felix Barrett, Punchdrunk artistic director[1]

"The 'spectator' in them must be awakened so that they perceive and enjoy the world of action around them…even as they function in it."

—Dorothy Heathcote, drama education teacher and scholar[2]

INTRODUCTION

The United Kingdom (UK) has emerged as an epicenter for innovation and experimentation in immersive theatre practices. From well-regarded and oft-documented companies like Shunt, Punchdrunk, CoLab, Coney, curious, and dreamthinkspeak, among others, to immersive productions *Ignition* and *Lifeguard* from the National Theatre of Scotland, to research and performances from Adam Alston, Mike Pearson, Josephine Machon, the late Adrian Howells, and Louise Ann Wilson, the immersive theatre movement is thriving in the UK. More importantly, these practices have increasingly international reach, particularly in the US. Thanks to Punchdrunk tours to Boston and New York, and new works by US companies like Third Rail, Dog and Pony, and Bricolage, increasingly, theatre artists and companies

---

[1] Kelly, Guy. "Punchdrunk Visionary Felix Barrett: 'If Audiences Get Used to the Rules, Change Them,'" June 19, 2015, sec. Culture. http://www.telegraph.co.uk/culture/culturenews/11675468/Punchdrunks-Felix-Barrett-If-audiences-get-used-to-the-rules-change-them.html.
[2] Heathcote, Dorothy, and Gavin M. Bolton. Drama for Learning: Dorothy Heathcote's Mantle of the Expert Approach to Education. Portmouth, NH: Heinemann, 1995. 18.

are taking cues from these pioneering UK companies and wrestling with the ideological, ethical, and aesthetic frameworks shaping this new genre.

As US-based theatre arts and scholars who focus on theatre for youth,[3] we are similarly fascinated and intrigued by the turn toward immersive theatre practices for two reasons. First, as this increasingly ubiquitous, but typically adult-centered, performance genre has flourished, young audiences have come into focus as potential target audiences.[4] For example, Punchdrunk has taken up young people as new audience for further experimentation in this genre, successfully producing its first immersive theatre piece specifically for children, *The Crash of the Elysium* in 2011 and followed with *Against Captain's Orders: A Journey into the Uncharted* in 2015. The company has also developed a comprehensive enrichment program and now teaches and facilitates Punchdrunk techniques with community groups and arts professionals. Of note for our field, Punchdrunk enrichment led master classes for attendees of TYA—USA's 2015 One Theatre World conference in Chicago, one of the largest gatherings for US theatre artists developing performances for young audiences. Other UK companies like Oily Cart, Kazzum (*Paper People*, 2015; the Immersive trilogy, 2008, 2012, 2014), Zest (*Gatecrash*, 2014; *Boy Meets Girl*, 2016), and even the National Theatre of Scotland (*The Day I Swapped My Dad For Two Goldfish*, 2013), among others, have all pioneered immersive work specifically for young audiences through the late 00s and 10s. Trickle-down effects of these conversations, education opportunities, and performance experiments have appeared in the US. A notable increase in both immersive pieces and immersive-esque pieces that include some qualities found in immersive theatre pieces have appeared in US theatre for youth in the last few years. Titles include Soho Repertory Theatre's *Washeteria* (2015), Trusty Sidekick's *Up and Away* (2015) and *The 7 1/2 Mysteries of Toulouse McLane* (2013–14), and Minneapolis Children's Theatre's *20,000 Leagues Under the Sea* (2015), to only scratch the surface. The sheer number of these new productions suggest that the immersive theatre zeitgeist has arrived stateside, leading many of us in the US who are interested in theatre for young people to think critically about and experiment with immersive theatre practices.

While the inclusion of young audiences in contemporary immersive theatre drives our interest, we have also been struck by resonances between practices adopted

---

[3] While we opt for the term "Theatre for Youth" to discuss this relatively young field, this usage should be considered in context with myriad other terms used to define the field of theatre with, by, and for young people in the US and UK. Drama in Education (DIE), synonymous with Creative Dramatics and improvisational drama, refers to process-oriented pedagogic drama without a formal presentation or performance of work. Theatre in Education (TIE), often situated under the larger heading of Applied Theatre, refers to formal productions including a large educational component, produced for and with young people for a specific pedagogic purpose (i.e. bullying, hygiene, racism, etcetera). Theatre for Young Audiences (TYA) refers to professional theatre by adults for children that include less explicit pedagogical goals, but which may have an aesthetic focus and often has both explicit and implicit educational components. All of these terms, along with several others including pedagogical drama and process drama, fall under the larger umbrella of "theatre for youth."

[4] Third Rail's Then She Fell, an adaptation of Lewis Carroll's Alice stories, revisits the author's adult-centered intent and allows no audience members under eighteen "due to liability issues." ("Frequently Asked Questions"). Likewise, audience members under sixteen are generally not admitted to Sleep No More.

for this path; breaking genre and the rich tradition of similar techniques adopted for pedagogical drama in classrooms and in theatre for youth (particularly from the UK traditions). Moreover, as recent scholarship and theatre-making has necessarily wrestled with theoretical and ideological complexities associated with defining the borders and contours of immersive theatre practice, less attention has been paid to the historical milieu that gave rise to the immersive theatre phenomenon. Out of necessity, scholars and artists have been much more concerned with questions of what immersive theatre *is* and *does* (and how we might likewise experiment and innovate with this genre) than with questioning and examining the unique historical and artistic influences that shaped this new form.

Accordingly, in this essay, we examine one potential and previously under-examined historical lineage for immersive theatre by considering the work of drama and theatre education pioneers who utilized many techniques also included in immersive theatre. These practitioners (Dorothy Heathcote, Peter Slade, and Brian Way) were a unique group who synthesized Progressive education trends, contemporary theatre practice, and movements in folk performance; creating original and process-oriented forms of performance pedagogy that directly involved the participants, most often children, in the creation and performance of theatrical work. Considering these artist/scholar/educators helps add nuance and complicate [sic] our historiographical understandings of immersive theatre practices in the contemporary era. However, this performance tradition has primarily existed outside larger discourses of theatre history and experimental theatre—given both its explicit focus on performance's pedagogical dimensions and its connection to amateur drama specifically with, by, and for children and young people. Despite this reality, there exist clear overlaps between this tradition and the contemporary immersive theatre phenomenon, as many of the same structures and methods used in contemporary immersive theatre practice also feature strongly in this pedagogical drama practice of the mid-twentieth century. They include use of in-role audience/performer interaction; open-ended narrative structures; ambulatory and promenade-style performance design; and heightened, highly interactive audience/performer exchange.

In the remainder of this essay, we place these drama teacher/artists' writings, methods, and artistic practices in conversation with extant scholarship and production histories of contemporary immersive theatre, highlighting connections and similarities between these two seemingly disparate performance genres. By connecting immersive theatre practices to performances created by these drama education pioneers, we demonstrate how a confluence of factors, including the impact of theatre for young people and pedagogically oriented drama, has supported the growth of immersive theatre as we understand it in this contemporary moment.

MACHINES, MARKETS, AND THE DEATH OF THE MASSES: DEFINING IMMERSIVE THEATRE

A discussion of immersive theatre's roots requires a substantive conversation regarding how scholars and artists have defined the genre thus far. Naturally, given both the amorphous, manifold nature of immersive theatre and its status as a genre coming into existence at the time in which we are crafting this essay, this task is complicated. Thus, we draw on extant scholarly investigations from Gareth White, Josephine Machon, and Adam Alston to contextualize our historical study while acknowledging that definitions are fluid and ever changing.

Immersive theatre's attributes spring from a synthesis of several artistic, ideological, and aesthetic traditions. Gareth White, an applied theatre practitioner, suggests that the historical roots of immersive theatre might be traced to the political participatory art of the 1960s, but the form has evolved away from an explicitly political orientation, leaving more room for aesthetic and thematic innovation. Through this evolution, White offers a working set of qualities and characteristics of immersive theatre, suggesting it is diverse in form, content and style while setting as a goal the reordering of audience/performer relationships via agency, participation, intimacy.[5] White also cites the theories of emancipated spectatorship as outlined by Rancière and theories of relational art as described by Bourriaud[6], describing immersive theatre as inextricably linked to engaged spectatorship. In extending and expanding White's discussion, Josephine Machon, leading scholar of immersive theatre practice, offers detailed descriptions of immersive theatre, defining "immersiveness, immersion, and immersivity" in her path-breaking monograph.[7] In her analysis, Machon arrives at the notion of "all-encompassing artistic experiences" and draws on the history of technologies, particularly gaming technologies, to mark the inclusion of "immersive" in discourses of performance.[8] Like White, Machon also engages with relational art theorists, including Bourriaud and Bishop, to connect with ideas of interactivity and empowered participation in spectatorship. She asserts immersive theatre is defined, at least in part, by "evolvement through involvement" whereby audiences become more than just spectators, but instead active participants in the making of performance—a kind of audience-plus. In this audience-plus paradigm, people attending immersive theatre performances are spectators first, but also collaborators. This act of collaboration with performers results in a new form of spectatorship that is empowered within theatrical and performative experiences.[9] Both White and Machon's discussions highlight the notion of an evolving spectator that is increasingly freed from traditional audience structures (sitting quietly, passively taking in the narrative, etcetera) and empowered within the theatrical event

In defining immersive theatre through these ideas about emancipated spectatorship and evolvement-through-involvement, Machon and White both stop short of asserting what specific conditions have necessitated this audience evolution. Adam Alston picks up these questions in his essay, considering immersive performance in the contemporary context of neoliberalism. He defines the participatory aspect of immersive audience-spectator experience as "entrepreneurial" in that it valorizes neoliberal principles like risk, agency, and personal

---

[5] White, Gareth. "On Immersive Theatre." Theatre Research International 37, no. 03 (October 2012): 221–35. doi:10.1017/S0307883312000880.
[6] Ibid. 222.
[7] Machon, Josephine. Immersive Theatres: Intimacy and Immediacy in Contemporary Performance. Palgrave Macmillan, 2013. 58–64.
[8] Ibid. 68–75.
[9] Ibid. 73.

responsibility.[10] This evocation of neoliberal economic practices as core influences in immersive theatre responds to both White and Machon's arguments about evolving audiences. By suggesting that theatre audiences, now immersed in the hyper-individualistic, technology-drenched neoliberal context of western post-modernity, require a role beyond passive spectatorship so often central to most theatrical performances, Alston offers another important contextualizing discussion regarding why immersive theatre has found such enthusiastic audiences. In effect, immersive theatre has directly responded to the contemporary cultural, political, and economic zeitgeist, producing art that both engages and entertains audiences through the increasingly novel world of live performance.

Taken together, these ideas, including the linkages with political participatory art, connections to interactive technologies and games, and the rise of neoliberal values, all present a compelling frame through which to think about immersive theatre and its relationship to theatrical innovation. Above all, these discussions suggest that immersive theatre sets out to redefine and reimagine relationships with audiences through experiments with engaged spectatorship—a chief defining quality we adopt for this essay. Engaging spectators may include a variety of different options, including opening opportunity for audience agency within dramatic, theatrical, and performative frameworks (exploring multiple performance sites that run in tandem as part of one performance event, presenting audiences with choices within dramatic narratives); shifting audience/performer relationships (one-on-one performances; heightened intimacy or extreme distancing with/from performers; sensory performances like auditory pieces run through headphones); and/or placing performance events settings that redefine theatrical spaces and audience orientations within them (site-specific performances, ambulatory/promenade performance). This definition, which we have deliberately left open, centers primarily on the theatre makers' artistic intent instead of how audiences respond to the performances as well, since predicting audience response is notoriously difficult. It also avoids siloing and taxonomizing immersive theatre practice, leaving room to consider a diversity of performance experiments as immersive, an especially important quality given the genre's nascence.

While keeping these influences and definitions in mind, we extend the conversation into the explicitly pedagogical and youth-centered realm, considering how genres of performance in this discipline, known as and/or in connection with participatory theatre, process drama, environmental drama, and drama in education, share many of the same characteristics of empowered and emancipated spectatorship lauded in theatre companies producing immersive work. As we proceed, we firmly acknowledge that tracing historical cause and effect is a thorny proposition, especially given the realities of an article's scope and the topic at hand. Thus, we center this conversation on a narrow window of time after World War I's end (roughly 1919) until the 1990s. Also, given connections between the UK as an epicenter for drama-in-education/theatre-in-education experimentation and as a similar site for immersive

---

[10] Alston, Adam. "Audience Participation and Neoliberal Value: Risk, agency and responsibility in immersive theatre." Performance Research 18, no. 2 (April 2013): 128. International Bibliography of Theatre and Dance with Full Text, EBSCOhost.

theatre experimentation, we primarily consider UK practitioners while acknowledging similar innovations occurred throughout the world. We do not set out to prove that immersive theatre practitioners were explicitly influenced by drama methods in schooling, but instead suggest the legacy of political participatory and folk art in both countries; the rise of neoliberal economic and cultural policy, most noted in the Thatcher and Reagan administrations of the 1980s; and, most importantly for this essay, the ubiquity of drama methods that overlap with immersive theatre practice in UK and US schools, community centers, and other sites of amateur and folk drama for young people supported immersive theatre's inception and subsequent growth.

MEN IN A MESS: THE PEDAGOGICAL ROOTS OF IMMERSIVE THEATRE PRACTICE

In looking at pedagogical drama—performance practices explicitly designed to engage participants in learning processes (as one potential influence in contemporary immersive theatre)–we acknowledge this genre typically falls outside records of theatre history, histories of education, and larger theoretical and artistic conversations about performance's evolution due to several factors. These factors include 1. Connections with children, 2. Connections with schools and schooling, 3. Connections to amateur and folk-art practice without explicit political aims, and 4. Its status as an inter- and trans-disciplinary performance genre that exists betwixt and between art and education. Thus, a brief contextualizing conversation of pedagogical drama frames the remainder of our essay.

First, distinguishing explicitly pedagogical drama from other dramatic forms is important. It is no [sic] overstatement to suggest that practically all theatre and performance genres are inherently pedagogical. Audiences and artists learn through performance creation and spectatorship; be it about values, aesthetics, ideologies, histories, or some other manifestation of knowledge. Moreover, connections between theatre and learning are long-standing and well documented. Theatrical performances, dramatic readings, and performative recitations have long been included in schooling and religious education throughout history, especially in the UK and US. At the same time, the impact and influence of theatre in educational settings are also oft-debated in these same contexts, a reality marked by Plato's objections to representational forms as corrupting influences in Book X of *The Republic* and continued today in discussions of school play censorship, the sanitization of dramatic narratives for children, and even protests of performances like *Angels in America*. As these examples demonstrate, theatre has long been a dangerous art, especially when it sets out to teach.

Despite the supposedly dangerous nature of pedagogical drama, artists and educators have continued to experiment with drama-based techniques in classroom contexts. This experimentation was particularly noteworthy in the US and UK and arose primarily from the advent and expansion of new philosophies about childhood and education, including Deweyean Progressivism, in the early part of the twentieth century. Specifically, John Dewey's writings on art, education, and experiential learning were a catalyst for new pedagogical drama practices. As one of the preeminent US philosophers writing in the late nineteenth century and first half of the twentieth century, Dewey's ideas about education transformed and continue [sic] to exert influence on the ways in which US and UK teachers and students teach and learn—especially in arts education fields. Nonetheless, this complex set of educational philosophies is effectively summarized by Dewey scholar Norman Dale Norris: "If we were to gather 100 of the brightest educational minds in this country and ask the question, 'What is Progressive education?' we might very likely get more than 100 different definitions, probably none of which could be considered necessarily right or wrong."[11] Despite the term's ambiguity, education Progressivists generally believe education should result in positive social change and progress forward as a society. In moving forward, the act of *doing* in the processes of both education and art-making were central to creating this change.

More specifically, Dewey believed that learning relied upon specific life relevancy—an act of doing or practicing doing. These principles extended to aesthetic experiences as well, whereby learners practiced skills in understanding and making art, a term Dewey deliberately left open for interpretation, as part of an education in real-life scenarios. These experiences would support learners as they cultivated understandings of life's aesthetic dimensions both in and beyond school. Dewey's synthesis of aesthetic education and experiential learning appear in his seminal work, *Art as Experience*, in which he critiques the tendency to "set Art upon a remote pedestal." He states: "In order to *understand* the esthetic [sic] in its ultimate and approved forms, one must begin with it in the raw; in the events and scenes that hold the attentive eye and ear of man, arousing his interest and affording him enjoyment as he looks and listens: the sights that hold the crowd..."[12] As outlined in this quote, Dewey believed authentic experiences with art rested with an individual's personal connection, or engagement, to aesthetic dimensions of life. While not explicitly referenced in many contemporary immersive theatre artists' writings, Deweyean philosophies about art resonate with sentiments from several immersive theatre-makers. For instance, in commenting on the philosophical underpinnings of his company's work, Punchdrunk's Felix Barrett articulates audience engagement as central to his company's creation of new pieces: "It was born from a desire to create work in which the audience is at the centre of the experience. We wanted to wrench them from the safety of traditional theatre seats and place them at the heart of the action, equipped with identity and purpose."[13] If acknowledging the ubiquity of Progressive philosophies in society, these ideas can be read as another influence, alongside neoliberalism, gaming, and explicitly political performance art, shaping immersive theatre's focus on emancipated and engaged spectatorship.

While Progressive education theories, as part of the twentieth century educational policy zeitgeist, influenced contemporary immersive theatre, Progressive philosophies about art and creativity explicitly inspired most of the pedagogical drama pioneers in

---

[11] Norris, Norman Dale. The Promise and Failure of Progressive Education. R&L Education, 2004. 9.

[12] Dewey, John. Art as Experience. New York: Minton, Balch & Company, 1934. 2–3.

[13] Wilson, Antonia. "The Drowned Man: An Interview with Immersive Theatre Masters Punchdrunk | Creative Review." 15 July 2015. Accessed January 6, 2016. https://www.creativereview.co.uk/cr-blog/2015/july/the-drowned-man-an-interview-with-immersive-theatre-masters-punchdrunk/.

the US and UK, along with many educators throughout the twentieth century's latter half. Likewise, these ideas directly contributed to experimentation with methods that look and feel very much like techniques employed in immersive theatre today. In the remainder of this essay, we consider three path-breaking UK practitioners and their techniques, demonstrating how closely contemporary immersive theatre practice aligns to many of these practices that have, for the most part, fallen outside of larger scholarly and artistic conversations about innovation in immersive theatre.

Peter Slade

While the tradition of incorporating immersive theatrical and dramatic methods into education can be traced back to several artists in the UK, the most prominent and influential is Peter Slade.[14] In the 1920s, Slade, an UK-based actor who also studied Jungian psychology, economics, and philosophy at the University of Bonn, became fascinated by the interplay between physical movement, drama, and young people, particularly in regards to drama's potential therapeutic and psychological effects. He is now regarded as a pioneer in drama therapy, child drama, and drama in education. Slade's seminal works, including *Child Drama* (1954), *An Introduction to Child Drama* (1958), *Experience of Spontaneity* (1968), and *Child Play* (1995), along with his training courses, professional presentations, and thirty-year tenure as drama advisor to the Birmingham Education Association, brought his ideas about performance to the fore [sic] of pedagogical drama practices.[15] Throughout his career, Slade emphasized the importance of play within process-oriented activities (as opposed to product-focused theatrical performance) in meaningful drama experiences for young people.[16] These principles grew out of Progressive education's focus on child-centered learning, a concept Slade extended to more fully conceive of young people as complex individuals in their own right who were, like adults, involved in complex processes of identity formation, exploration, and social and personal development.[17] He deemed this "child-concerned" philosophy of learning as vital to both young people's mental health and their social development. He also staunchly supported process-oriented drama as a central method in support of this kind of authentic, engaged learning.

Slade's child-concerned philosophies and techniques, which he pioneered in the UK between 1930 and 1970, connect with immersive theatre in the contemporary era through shared values of engaged and emancipated spectatorship. While immersive theatre-makers have been lauded for opening up the spectator experience and giving audiences a part to play within the performance, Slade considered participant engagement central to meaningful drama experiences decades before the immersive theatre appeared. In describing these practices, Slade offers the following:

---

[14] See also the work of Harriet Finlay-Johnson, Caldwell Cook, and Richard Courteney, among others.
[15] *Anthony Jackson (1990). "Archives Of An Educational Drama Pioneer: A Survey Of The Peter Slade Collection In The John Rylands University Library Of Manchester. "*Bulletin of the John Rylands Library 72 (2):153.
[16] Slade, Peter. Child Drama. London: University of London Press, 1954.
[17] Slade, Peter. "Peter Slade Talks." Research In Drama Education 4, no. 2 (September 1999): 253. International Bibliography of Theatre & Dance with Full Text, EBSCOhost (accessed January 5, 2016).

"In drama— i.e. doing and struggling— the child discovers life and self through emotional and physical attempt...the experiences are exciting and personal, and can develop into group experience. But in neither the personal nor the group experience is there any consideration of theatre in the adult sense, *unless we impose it*. There may be intense moments of what we would deign to call theatre, but in the main it is drama, the adventure, doing, questing, and struggling are tried by all. All are doers, both actor and audience, going where they wish and facing any direction they like during play."[18]

This quote, published in Slade's 1958 book, *Child Drama*, both highlights engagement's significance in dramatic experiences and advocates for blurring distinctions between actor and audience, between watcher and doer, and between play and performance. These same principles are celebrated in contemporary immersive theatre. However, contemporary artists, afforded more than sixty years of further study about human development, have capitalized on the notion that play continues to hold relevance in people's lives, even as they move into adulthood. Productions like *Sleep No More* and *Then She Fell* provide audiences a chance to "do, quest, and struggle" as a form of dramatic play within the context of a formal theatrical performance.

While Slade centered his research and art practice exclusively on children, a reality shaped by the growing fields of developmental and educational psychology and childhood studies during the first half of the twentieth century, his path-breaking theories and methods for process-oriented, play-centered drama influenced many other practitioners, particularly after World War II. These practitioners further expanded and developed his ideas, generating new methodological and philosophical schools of thought, and helped shaped this nascent performance discipline by exploring possibilities inherent to playing with boundaries between process-oriented drama and theatrical productions experienced by audiences.

Brian Way

One of the most prominent figures in the continued development of these process-oriented drama methods was Brian Way. Way, a theatre artist, playwright, theorist, and teacher, regularly collaborated with Slade. The two shared an interest in developing and refining methods for drama-based learning. However, while Slade shifted his work more toward drama therapy, adapting theatrical methods to support young people's mental and social health, Way focused on formal theatrical productions for children. In 1953, Way founded the Theatre Centre, one of the UK's most prominent and path-breaking theatre for youth companies. At this point in time, the most prominent London-based company producing theatrical works for young people was the Unicorn Theatre. The Unicorn set out to provide high-quality productions that were as aesthetically and thematically sophisticated as theatrical

---

[18] Slade, Peter. An Introduction to Child Drama. London: University of London Press, 1958. 2.

works for adults.[19] While laudable, the Unicorn's high-art-for-kids approach did not appeal to Way, and he opted for a contrasting aesthetic, developing bare-bones touring productions that were intimate, pedagogically oriented, and, above all, participatory.

While testing out new ideas and developing new works (he wrote and produced over fifty new plays), Way crafted two important books that moved forward conversations about immersive drama methods. In the first, *Development through Drama* (1967), Way extended ideas presented by Slade and contemporaries by advocating for drama as a key method to develop [sic] the whole child. For Way, developing the whole child included not only her intellect, but also her emotions, imagination, and senses, among other qualities.[20] Like Slade, Way believed drama was ideal for engaging learners in this holistic form of education given its connection with the study of individuality. As Way states, "Education is concerned with individuals; drama is concerned with the individuality of individuals."[21] This quote highlights the significance Way attached to individualized and personalized experience in drama work. Thus, his repertoire of process-oriented drama techniques, where participants immersed themselves in imagined and improvised scenarios through physical engagement, imagination, and critical thinking, helped learners develop both a sense of self and an empathic understanding of others. Instead of passively taking in a lesson or performing for an audience in order to communicate ideas, participants in Way's approach to drama meaningfully engaged within dramatic contexts with little attention paid to formal theatrical structures found in other more traditional productions like those offered by the Unicorn. Also, Way's description of drama as an individualized performance practice that explores what makes individuals unique foreshadows the aforementioned commentary from Adam Alston regarding the entrepreneurial audience experience offered by many successful contemporary immersive theatre pieces.

In addition to his philosophical and practical writings about why and how teachers and artists might integrate drama practices into their work with children, Way also wrote extensively about participatory theatre practices for young people. In his 1981 book, *Audience Participation*, Way describes audience participation as an innate "phenomenon" in performances for children, largely because young audiences have not been fully inculcated into passive audience structures that discourage verbal and physical engagement as part of spectatorship.[22] Way celebrates this reality, describing various methods by which theatre-makers might encourage participation from young audiences. For example, Way strongly encourages theatre-makers to eschew the proscenium theatre arrangement and explore "open staging" that supports closer connections between actors and audiences. He describes several set-ups based on his Theatre Centre productions that support a more intimate engagement between

---

[19] As described in the company's history, the founding philosophy stated, "'the best of theatre for children should be judged on the same high standards of writing, directing, acting and design as the best of adult theatre." (*https://www.unicorntheatre.com/about-us*)

[20] Way, Brian. Development through Drama. 13.

[21] Ibid. 3

[22] 1–2.

performer and spectator.[23] Way also advocated for different styles of participation, including immersion into dramatic narratives, in which audience members (especially older teen audiences) take on roles, offer solutions to conflicts, and generate new scenarios within the dramatic narrative that the actors would improvisationally [sic] integrate into their performance. Way's examination of audience participation not only presents several clear techniques for immersing audiences into theatrical productions, but also demonstrates his interest in negotiating the interplay between "the process of drama" and "the product of theatre" in his works. Way, even more so than Slade, was constantly experimenting with ways in which to balance young audiences' experiences within both a dramatic process and a formal theatrical product. His ideas were widely received; throughout the 1970s and 1980s, Way's techniques garnered increased attention, particularly from artists and educators associated with the explicitly pedagogical Theatre in Education (TIE) movement and theatre artists creating participatory plays beyond the UK's borders.[24] Theatre artists like Moses Goldberg and the members of New York City's Creative Arts Team, one of the first US TIE companies, among others, all took inspiration from Way's approach, innovating new techniques and producing new kinds of participatory art for young people. As this discussion points out, Way paved a way for new conversations about how formal theatrical production might engage and emancipate audience members, a conversation still ongoing amongst immersive theatre-makers today.

Dorothy Heathcote

While Slade and Way's contributions to immersive drama methods are significant, UK drama educator/artist Dorothy Heathcote's techniques are also pivotal in shaping these practices, particularly in regards to developing immersive experiences for groups. Heathcote, an actress, teacher and academic, pioneered many roleplay and process-oriented drama techniques now adapted for pedagogical drama work in theatre for youth. She is famous for referring to drama as "men in a mess." As the quote suggests, Heathcote focused much more on collective experiences, empowering groups to engage together in dramatic narratives and scenarios. Her ideas contrast with Slade and Way, who were focused on individual exploration and personal development through drama processes. She introduced many techniques for immersive drama practice, with the most prominent being Mantle of the Expert (MoE).[25] In MoE, a series of techniques Heathcote developed to support facilitators and communities with little experience in theatre as an artistic discipline, a group of

---

[23] Ibid. 65–80.

[24] The unique UK TIE model, professional and participatory theatre productions performed by professional actors that set out to teach an explicit message, is considered one important historical root for the larger contemporary Applied Theatre movement. See John O'Toole's Theatre in Education: New Objectives for Theatre, New Techniques in Education, Julianna Saxton and Monica Predergast's Applied Theatre: International Case Studies and Challenges for Practice, Roger Wooster's Contemporary Theatre in Education, and Tim Prentki and Sheila Preston's The Applied Theatre Reader for additional information on TIE.

[25] See Heathcote and Bolton's Drama for Learning: Dorothy Heathcote's Mantle of the Expert Approach to Education for additional description.

learners (for instance, a sixth-grade class) are presented with a challenge or problem and assigned fictional roles to try and solve the task. The MoE experience is both loosely structured and highly engaging based on participants' needs and desires. Activities might include improvisations, town meetings, research, presentations, or any other activity deemed useful in the imagined context of the fictional MoE world. Within this method, the teacher or facilitator is likewise empowered to participate both in- and out-of-role, moving forward the work, and when appropriate, challenging participants, and stepping out of role as needed to clarify and process both activities and larger thematics inherent to the work. In the now-famous documentary about her work, *Three Looms Waiting*, Heathcote demonstrates early versions of this work with a group of pre-adolescent boys.[26] The MoE situation the group selects, British soldiers breaking out of a German POW camp, is high-stakes, particularly for participants only a few decades removed from World War II. Heathcote likewise invests in the drama with shocking fervor, fully embodying her role as the maleficent enemy officer who disarms the soldiers and imprisons them, thus starting the drama. The young participants are fully engaged and completely in-role, strategizing ways to break out, growing angry with one another, and ultimately discovering a traitor among them who prevents their escape—men in a mess, indeed.

Heathcote's techniques, including MoE, signify another progression in the larger project of experimenting with process and product in immersive pedagogical drama. Heathcote comments directly on this interplay in a description of MoE's philosophical underpinnings. She describes the process as "deep social (and sometimes personal) play"—since participants "contract into fiction" and "understand the power they have within that fiction to direct, decide, and function."[27] Like Slade, Heathcote also evokes the seriousness of engaged play in successful dramatic work. In addition, Heathcote presents the idea of audience/participants holding process and product simultaneously as they engage with the dramatic situation presented before them: "the 'spectator' in them must be awakened so that they perceive and enjoy the world of action around them...even as they function in it."[28] This description of participants functioning as spectators-plus echoes both Josephine Machon's earlier discussion of the engaged and emancipated spectator in contemporary immersive theatre and many of the philosophies of contemporary immersive theatre-makers.

Together, Slade, Way, and Heathcote provide a noteworthy body of knowledge about immersive theatre practice in schools and for young people. Their path-breaking ideas and methods about immersive theatre have inspired countless other artists and educators to experiment with process-oriented drama with young people. Their works have been translated into several other languages, and all three are held up as key figures in understanding how drama might operate as a method in immersive and engaged learning processes.

---

[26] Heathcote, Dorothy, British Broadcasting Corporation, Television Service, and Time-Life Films. Three Looms Waiting. Paramus, N.J: distributed by Time-Life Films, 1978.
[27] Heathcote, Dorothy, Liz Johnson, Cecily O'Neill, and Jonathan Levy. Dorothy Heathcote: Collected Writings on Education and Drama. Evanston, Ill: Northwestern University Press, 1991.18.
[28] Ibid.

CONCLUSION

While contemporary immersive theatre-makers have not, to our knowledge, explicitly identified Slade, Way, and Heathcote as influences on their art, they benefit from a cultural and educational fabric shaped by these artist/educator pioneers. Slade, Way, and Heathcote's work represents only a fraction of the artistic experimentation, often conducted by teachers, amateur drama groups, and community organizations in school classrooms, church basements, and summer camps, that blurred lines between audience and actor and between play and performance. By their nature, many of these experiments were process-oriented and explicitly focused on amateur audiences and participants, and thus have not received the same level of documentation afforded other professional, adult-centered theatrical experiments. Nonetheless, this work, perhaps more than formal productions, shaped countless young people's understandings of the many and varied ways that art might manifest in life. As children discovered that actors and audiences might interact during a performance or that supposedly good audience behavior might also involve moving bodies and vocalizing ideas, or even that experiencing theatre may be more about play and less about quietly comprehending a moral message, they also likely opened their minds toward new possibilities for making performance as well. Moreover, as theatre-makers continue to experiment and innovate in the immersive theatre genre, both for adults and young people, they might benefit from considering some of the artists and methods detailed here when planning successful audience immersion. By attending to performance forms that exist on the margins of our dominant discourses about art and innovation, including those that are both explicitly pedagogical and oriented toward young people as discussed here, we shed light on the wider context surrounding the creation and expansion of immersive theatre.

BIBLIOGRAPHY

Dewey, John. *Art as Experience*. New York: Minton, Balch & Company, 1934.

Dillon, David A., and Brian Way. "Perspectives: Drama as a Sense of Wonder-Brian Way." *Language Arts* 58, no. 3 (1981): 356–62.

"Frequently Asked Questions." *Then She Fell*. Accessed December 9, 2015. http://www.thenshefell.com/ticket-info/.

Heathcote, Dorothy, and Gavin M. Bolton. *Drama for Learning: Dorothy Heathcote's Mantle of the Expert Approach to Education*. Dimensions of Drama. Portmouth, NH: Heinemann, 1995.

Heathcote, Dorothy, British Broadcasting Corporation, Television Service, and Time-Life Films. *Three Looms Waiting*. Paramus, N.J: distributed by Time-Life Films, 1978.

Heathcote, Dorothy, Liz Johnson, Cecily O'Neill, and Jonathan Levy. *Dorothy Heathcote: Collected Writings on Education and Drama*. Evanston, Ill: Northwestern University Press, 1991.

"Is Theatre Becoming Too Immersive?" n.d. http://www.independent.co.uk/arts-entertainment/theatre-dance/features/is-theatre-becoming-too-immersive-8521511.html.

Jackson, Anthony. Archives of an Educational Drama Pioneer: A Survey of the Peter Slade.

Collection in the John Rylands University Library of Manchester. Manchester, 1990.

Kelly, Guy. "Punchdrunk Visionary Felix Barrett: 'If Audiences Get Used to the Rules, 'Change Them,'" June 19, 2015, sec. Culture. http://www.telegraph.co.uk/culture/culturenews/11675468/Punchdrunks-Felix-Barrett-If-audiences-get-used-to-the-rules-change-them.html.

Machon, Josephine. Immersive Theatres: Intimacy and Immediacy in Contemporary *Performance*. Palgrave Macmillan, 2013.

Norris, Norman Dale. The Promise and Failure of Progressive Education. R&L Education, 2004.

O'Toole, John. Theatre in Education: New Objectives for Theatre, New Techniques in Education. Hodder and Stoughton, 1976.

Prendergast, Monica, and Juliana Saxton. Applied Theatre: International Case Studies and Challenges for Practice. Intellect Books, 2009.

Prentki, Tim, and Sheila Preston. *The Applied Theatre Reader*. Routledge, 2013.

Slade, Peter. *An Introduction to Child Drama*. London: University of London Press, 1958.

———.Child Play: Its Importance for Human Development. London: J. Kingsley Publishers, 1995.

———. *Experience of Spontaneity*. London: Longmans, 1969.

———. *Child Drama*. London: University of London Press, 1954.

———. "Peter Slade Talks." *Research in Drama Education: The Journal of Applied Theatre and Performance* 4, no. 2 (September 1, 1999): 253–57. doi:10.1080/1356978990040210.

"The Drowned Man: An Interview with Immersive Theatre Masters Punchdrunk | Creative Review." Accessed January 6, 2016. blog/2015/july/the-drowned-man-an-interview-with-immersive-theatre-masters-punchdrunk/.

Way, Brian. Audience Participation: Theatre for Young People. Boston, MA: W.H. Baker, 1981.

———. *Development through Drama*. Atlantic Highlands, N.J.: Humanities Press, 1967.

White, Gareth. "On Immersive Theatre." *Theatre Research International* 37, no. 03 (October 2012): 221–35. doi:10.1017/S0307883312000880.

Wilson, Antonia. "The Drowned Man: An Interview with Immersive Theatre Masters Punchdrunk | Creative Review." 15 July 2015. Accessed January 6, 2016. https://www.creativereview.co.uk/cr-blog/2015/july/the-drowned-man-an-interview-with-immersive-theatre-masters-punchdrunk/.

Wooster, Roger. *Contemporary Theatre in Education*. Intellect Books, 2007.

CHAPTER 8

Milk *Does* the Body

Jaclyn Meloche

A hot summer night in July 2006. Me, an emerging performance artist, along with a friend, colleague, and art enthusiast, walk into the Ontario College of Art and Design Professional Art Gallery in downtown Toronto to attend the opening reception for Jess Dobkin's controversial performance *The Lactation Station Breast Milk Bar*, organized by Paul Couillard.[1] The room is white, stark, cold and crowded. A man wearing a tuxedo carrying a silver platter greets us at the door. He first offers us a menu, and then a shot of milk. He, among a group of servers circulating around the room, offers colourfully named samples of breast milk.[2] Once he introduces all six varieties, he explains that each of the sample's colors, flavors, smells and tastes are different depending on the body that they came from.

My friend eagerly takes a shot—"not bad," she says. I, on the other hand, am unable to indulge in this experience. Already uncomfortable with the idea of breastfeeding, I am gripped by nausea, feeling faint, and truthfully a little ashamed. I feel that my refusal to drink is written all over my face. Worse, I feel as though I am the only person in the room who feels this particular kind of discomfort. Did this make me a bad person? A bad woman? Or worse, does it mean that I will make a bad mother one day? Overwhelmed by so many insecurities, I still have yet to be able to forget this experience. Today, nearly ten years later, why am I still preoccupied with this performance? Moreover, how did this experience of performance art change the ways in which I myself understand and practice performance, as well as write about performance?

---

[1] According to Curator Charles Reeve from the Ontario College of Art and Design Professional Art Gallery in Toronto, Canada, controversy follows the Toronto-based performance artist Jess Dobkin. In his essay "The Kindness of Human Milk: Jess Dobkin's Lactation Station Breast Milk Bar," Reeve situates the performance within a long history of controversial acts performed by Dobkin; "[s]tirring the pot of controversy comes easily to Dobkin, who, for more than a decade, has infused her performances with sex and humour. Her early piece Eat Out (1996) introduced food into this mix by capping an evening of performance and dining with "a live cunt-eating contest for dessert." Charles Reeve, "The Kindness of Human Milk: Jess Dobkin's Lactation Station Breast Milk Bar." Gastronomica. Winter 2009, 70.

[2] Six women donated breast milk for pasteurization and sampling. Each sample was listed on a tasting menu under a specific name: Passion's Legacy, Sweet Fall Harvest, Life Force Elixir, Temple of the Goddess, Straight Up with a Twist and Truth Serum #9. The Lactation Station Breast Milk Bar Tasting Menu. Courtesy of the artist. April 10, 2014.

The Lactation Station Breast Milk Bar was unlike any performance, or event, that I had yet to encounter. Until that evening, I saw performance art as a medium in which bodies performed. Whether on stage, in a gallery, or in public, performance artists acted, reenacted, read, sang, or protested their work for an audience to witness. But this was different. I didn't know who the artist was or who the mothers were, but nor [sic] did I need to know. In fact, these details were insignificant. From the moment that I entered the space, the only performer who physically, psychologically, and materially did onto me was the milk. Like actors, each shot glass performed my body, my mind, and my behavior through my refusal to consume the white liquid.

Through a curatorial lens, the representation of milk in contemporary art is more commonly considered within what architectural historian and art critic Kenneth Hayes refers to as a "milk-splash discourse"—a field of inquiry that grew out of the California Pop Art scene in the early 1960s to negotiate the ways in which milk becomes a metaphor for the human body; "[t]he milk-splash discourse problematized the identity of the white fluid to the point at which it could no longer, with any certainty, be identified as milk."[3] Recalling the maternal body, infancy, nourishment, the domestic body, the sexual body, semen excretion and conception, Hayes explains that contemporary depictions of milk, particularly in photography, speak to larger ideas of commodification and consumption, particularly in works by artists such as Jeff Wall, Ed Ruscha, Gilbert and George, and General Idea.

Through milk imagery, or rather milk splashes, Hayes' male-dominated case studies collectively complicate the active, or rather agential, nature of milk by capitalizing on its photographic stillness. Through performance, Dobkin in comparison, perpetuates the substance's movement and material agency by showcasing its liveness in the art gallery. By trivializing the distinctions between body-as-performer and material-as-performer, Dobkin instigates an unconventional method of engaging with performance art by blurring the distinctions between body and subject. In comparison to the body-centric genre of performance that I had become accustomed to, *The Lactation Station* [sic] showcases a shift in the ways in which subject and body interact in a performance situation.

In parallel to feminist quantum physicist Karen Barad's model of post-humanist performativity in which nonhuman matter begins to matter through intra-activity, Dobkin is complicating the human/nonhuman dichotomy that is inherent to feminist post-humanist discourses. Moreover, through pasteurization and distribution, the artist materially and theoretically displaces all agency, what Barad parallels with a form of inherent doing,[4] from the body and, through performance, and inserts it into the breast milk. Therefore, unlike traditional forms of art criticism that deploy iconography as a starting point for the visual analysis of food in art, this example moves beyond the boundaries of formal analysis by considering instead the posthuman aesthetics of a substance—the embodied qualities that transform a nonhuman subject into an agent.

---

[3] Kenneth Hayes, Milk and Melancholy. (Toronto and Cambridge: Prefix Institute of Contemporary Art, MIT Press, 2008), 153.

[4] "Agency is 'doing' or 'being' in its intra-activity. It is the enactment of iterative changes to particular practices-iterative reconfigurings of topological manifolds of spacetime-matter relations-through the dynamics of intra-activity." Karen Barad, Meeting the Universe Halfway: Quantum Physics and the Entanglement of Matter and Meaning. (London: Duke University Press, 2007), 178.

In traditional art historical [sic] discourses, food art is often interpreted through a Panofsky-inspired iconographic lens. According to art historian Travis Nygard, food-related imagery in Renaissance and modern painting can only be considered within the politics of iconography because food, historically, reveals a variety of symbolic and semiotic functions in visual culture.[5]

Limited in theory and practice, iconography, in Western art history, does not address a work of art's context. Nor does it consider the occurrence of an experience, albeit a human or a material experience. Rather, according to the German art historian Erwin Panofsky, art can only truthfully be deconstructed through iconography; "[i]t is possible to experience every object, natural or man-made, aesthetically. We do this, to express it as simply as possible, when we just look at it (or listen to it) without relating it, intellectually or emotionally, to anything outside of itself."[6] In other words, to understand an image, and its relationship to the viewer, is to understand art.

Riddled with limitations, this particular methodology does very little for the interpretation of food in art. In comparison to Panofsky and his contemporary Nygard, who both argue that iconography is the only method of analysis suitable for describing the social, contextual, and political situations of food imagery in art,[7] a deconstruction based on aesthetics in fact ghettoizes food into an economic and Marxist sign rather than understanding the ways in which it becomes a source of power.

In early Renaissance painting, for example, food imagery was often considered a sign of wealth—the artist's wealth, the patron's wealth, and the sitter's wealth in a portrait. In Jan van Eyck's painting *The Arnolfini Portrait* (also known as *The Arnolfini Wedding*, and/or *The Portrait of Giovanni Arnolfini and his Wife*) (1434), the clementines grouped on the table behind the male figure indicate a level of wealth because fresh fruit during this time period was a luxury. When considered within the traditions of iconography, the oranges, however, become limited to class signifiers, over material objects and thus, get lost in the perils of Marxist representation.

When drawing from Karen Barad's model of post humanist performativity, an analysis of food imagery [in art] moves beyond an iconographical discourse of representation entering instead into a realm of socio-political commentary by way of a Marxist interpretation of food and culture. Framed within a space in which materials begin to *matter* through intra-activity, breast milk is not limited to a human bi-product that nourishes the body.

Likened to the active agents pursued by science studies, breast milk in Dobkin's performance, becomes a participant, or rather what historian Rebecca Herzig refers to

---

[5] Travis Nygard, "Food and Art" in Albala, Ken. Ed. Routledge International Handbook of Food Studies. (London and New York: Routledge, 2013), 171.

[6] Erwin Panofsky, "The History of Art as a Humanistic Discipline." (1940) In Art History and Its Methods: A Critical Anthology. Eric Fernie. Ed. (London: Phaidon Press, 1995), 190.

[7] "A food-related iconological analysis might strive to understand whether it is important that the rolls of bread on the table are shown uneaten, that empty plates and bowls are shown carefully placed in front of disciples, that wine glasses are all shown half full, that some fruits and vegetables are shown scattered on the tablecloth, and that two platters appear to contain the main course. The scholar would ultimately argue that the artist used the biblical text as a starting point, but that the painting also represents a new understanding of food geared toward the patron and viewer," Nygard, 171.

as an actor, entangled within what John Law names *relational materiality*, "[f]or such actors, agency is not a predetermined condition or capacity, but instead the mutable effect of *relational materiality*."[8] In addition to being done by the body, breast milk, in this performance, does onto the body; it informs the choreography of the event, as well as the ways in which each body interacts. Through a post humanist performative lens, milk's material agency becomes apparent, its tastes, smells, colors, and cheeky identities in the performance influences the viewer-turned-participant's body to feel, react, and respond differently to other bodies in the gallery, including their own body.

PERFORMATIVITY WITHIN PERFORMANCE STUDIES

The material shifts between performance and the performative in *The Lactation Station Breast Milk Bar* are not only exemplified through the subject of the event, the milk, but also through the ways in which the material interacts with and through the body. The participants in this event fluctuate between the artists, the women who donated breast milk, the servers, the spectators, as well as the invisible bodies of the babies. Collectively, each body in the space of the gallery, through ingestion, digestion, and voyeurism become done onto by the milk, as well as continually do onto each other through their interactions with the material.

Regardless of each participant's ingestion of breast milk, the material's agency continues to *matter* through each person's consideration to drink, or not. For example, although I did not consume breast milk during my visit, its embodied agency still affected and effected the ways in which I moved, felt, and interacted with other bodies in the gallery.

To aesthetically complement the performativity of breast milk in the performance, the artist re-designed the art gallery into a cocktail bar. Decorated with a large white shag rug, white leather lounge chairs, a white bar lined with white bar stools, the gallery transformed into a club-like venue where spectators were met by servers offering milk 'shots' on silver platters. However, this so-called change was not only aesthetic. The artist no longer was represented as the sole creative producer in the piece, but rather became one of many performers. As active agents during the event, the spectators transformed into subjects as well as participants by drinking, socializing, and mingling with the crowd. Through what performance studies scholars identify as the occurrence of *transformance*, Dobkin's identity becomes blurred and arguably *transformed* during the event of the performance. Leading to questions, such as who, or what, becomes the creative agent? Or, who embodies the role of performer? The occurrence of transformance results in a complete recontextualization of the event.

According to performance theorist Richard Schechner, the occurrence of transformance is at the heart of performance. Akin to German theatre and performance studies historian Erika Fischer-Lichte, whose argument that performance is the result of an experiential exchange, Schechner, too, favors the concept that performance, or what he terms drama, is rooted in dialogical acts of being. For instance, he explains that performance is a procedural medium that can inspire and

---

[8] Rebecca Herzig, "On Performance, Productivity and Vocabularies of Motive in Recent Studies of Science." Feminist Theory. 2004, 134.

manifest change; that "[a]s in all rites of passage something had happened during the performance. The performance both symbolized and actualized the change in status."[9] Similar to a braid in which independent elements are overlapped and entangled to create a whole, performance is "…a mixture, a braid, of entertainment and ritual."[10] Embedded within a modernist approach to theater is Schechner's model for framing the experiential. To perform is to be, and that meaning is born from an ensemble of experiences that when brought together create consciousness.

In a comparison between the body and things in theater, Schechner inserts a clear binary between who, or what, arguably matters on stage, or in a rehearsal room. Yet by proposing that there is a distinction between the ways in which scientists and artists understand and *do* performance (scientists through observation and artists through experience), Schechner neglects to consider the ways in which observation and experience become entangled methods of producing a subject's meaning, as well as its ability to do. Evident of Bohr's argument that the scientist is only ever an observer, and never a participant, Schechner's analysis of the performing artist exemplifies the ways in which the body in performance continually transforms into a psychophysical entanglement. In other words, a performing artist, according to Schechner, becomes the result of its embodied transformance.

The debate between what and what not [sic] counts as performative is a problematic [sic] that Karen Barad complicates by blurring the aesthetic and agential functions of performative matter. Reminiscent of the traditions of performance studies in which the body has historically been assigned sole agency, Barad negotiates the relationship between material matter and human matter while also assessing the physical and physiological experience of materiality vis-à-vis the body.

In Schechner's analogy that performativity is rooted in the experiential exchange between the body and the stage, he explains that "…the performance the spectators see—is the visible result of a trialog among: 1) the conventions or givens of a genre, 2) the stretching, distorting, or invention of new conventions, and 3) brain-centered psychophysical transformations of self."[11] In other words, performance, in the context of theatre, represents the result of the body's relationships with its environment. By framing the event of a performance as a model for communicative exchange, Schechner argues that to perform means to enact a change and transformation among its participants.

For example, the spectator, according to his analysis, is an active participant whose identity is continually redefined in theater. Whether they become participants in the space of the event, or they undergo a private and experiential transformation, they inevitably leave the theatre a changed person. Influenced by the anthropologist Victor Turner's work on social drama, Schechner interprets the spectator according to two models: the aesthetic drama and the social drama. However, he also believes that drama is the result of a transformation, albeit one that is rooted in human consciousness while the other is physical.

---

[9] Richard Schechner, Performance Theory. (London and New York: Routledge, 1988), 127.
[10] Ibid. 162.
[11] Ibid. 321.

PERFORMATIVITY VERSUS POST-HUMANIST PERFORMATIVITY

In contrast to Schechner's anthropocentric positioning of performance as rooted in a human psychological self, Karen Barad, in her feminist-inspired research in quantum physics, argues that everything in the world, albeit human or nonhuman, *matters*, culture *matters*, language *matters*, and things *matter*. Troubled by the ways in which structuralism has historically and philosophically determined who, or what *matters* according to systems of binary oppositions, such as nature/culture, man/woman, and human/nonhuman, Barad's theories of performativity are intended to challenge the belief that linguistic and semiotic representations of meaning vis-à-vis Being fail to explain how things begin to matter.

More specifically, "[a] *performative* understanding of discursive practices challenges the representationalist belief in the power of words to represent preexisting things. Unlike representationalism, which positions us above or outside of the world we allegedly merely reflect on, a performative account insists on understanding thinking, observing, and theorizing as practices of engagement with, and as part of, the world in which we have our being."[12] Performativity thus challenges linguistic systems of material description and representation by proposing that a thing's being is instead informed by its actions, and doings.

In her attempt to answer the overarching question *how does matter come to matter,* Barad disentangles the ways in which to understand being, doing, acting, and interacting vis-à-vis material agency. For example, to understand that matter does is to understand that matter is active—a term Barad associates with agentive.[13] And if matter is agentive, then it literally and philosophically translates into a form of material agency, which through intra-activity, becomes a framework through which to destabilize and re-conceptualize matter as ultimately agential rather than representational. In other words, material agency becomes a method through which to understand how matter begins to *matter*. According to Barad, "[t]he notion of *intra-action* (in contrast to the usual "interaction," which presumes the prior existence of independent entities/relata) represents a profound conceptual shift. It is through specific agential intra-actions that the boundaries and properties of the "components" of phenomena become determinate and that particular embodied concepts become meaningful."[14]

In her effort to complicate the inherent limitations of representationalism, a discourse that she claims limits the meaning of matter to language, Barad proposes to consider the latter through a post-humanist performative lens, a scientific framework in which matter *becomes* matter through intra-activity. In essence, she argues that material matter is not self-referential, but rather inter-active, communicative, and

---

[12] Barad, (2007), 133.

[13] "Matter is neither fixed and given nor the mere end result of different processes. Matter is produced and productive, generated and generative. Matter is agentive, not a fixed essence or property of things. Mattering is differentiating, and which differences come to matter, matter in the iterative production of different differences." Barad, (2007), 137.

[14] Karen Barad, (2003), "Post humanist Performativity: Toward an Understanding of How Matter Comes to Matter." In Material Feminisms. Stacy Alaimo and Susan Hekman. Ed. (Bloomington and Indianapolis: Indiana University Press, 2008), 133.

agential through its intra-relational and *intra-active* exchange with the body; "[m]atter is therefore not to be understood as a property of things but, like discursive practices, must be understood in more dynamic and productive terms, in terms of intra-activity."[15]

Originally rooted in linguistics and semiotics, the word doing in relationship to performance was used by John L. Austin in his critique of the predominant at the time reign [sic] of natural language theory, to suggest that words, upon their utterance, *do* something; that words embody power, and therefore when spoken, become their truth. In a series of lectures at Harvard University in 1955 entitled *How to Do Things With Words*, Austin proposed to name these words "performatives," words that, in essence, perform their meaning through their doing, "[t]he term 'performative' will be used in a variety of cognate ways and constructions, much as the term 'imperative' is. The name is derived, of course, from 'perform', the usual verb with the noun 'action': it indicates that the issuing of the utterance is the performing of an action."[16]

In comparison to Austin's theory of performativity, Barad's entanglement of science studies and feminism challenges the power that has historically been attributed to language. Through a materially-discursive method of iterative enactment, or rather post humanist performativity, matter thus becomes the result of its practices, doings, and actions; "[t]he world is a dynamic process of intra-activity and materialization in the enactment of determinate causal structures with determinate boundaries, properties, meanings, and patterns of marks on bodies."[17]

MILK, MATERIAL AGENCY, AND THING-POWER

In the context of Jess Dobkin's performance *The Lactation Station Breast Milk Bar*, breast milk marked bodies. It coated digestive systems, it navigated the body in space, and it even repulsed the body—my body. Through Barad's model of post-humanist performativity, milk, in this case study, becomes a prime example of material agency vis-à-vis post-humanist performativity. With reference to science studies and postfeminist inquiry, Dobkin's so-called lead actor embodies the ability to *do* in the performance transforming it into a material agent that is active, participatory, and ultimately performative.

Yet, by contextualizing material matter as an actant that co-exists and co-performs with and by the body, Barad echoes the political theorist Jane Bennett who proposes an alternative for reading matter as transformative; "...an actant never really acts alone. Its efficacy or agency always depends on the collaboration, cooperation, or interactive interference of many bodies and forces."[18] Subsequently, that [sic] the transformative power of performance occurs through a reciprocal interaction between two or more 'things'. In attempting to understand the manner in which things themselves can act as material agents, Bennett describes what she calls "thing-power," which proposes to complicate the binaries that distinguish between thing and human;

---

[15] Barad, (2007), 150.

[16] John L. Austin, How To Do Things With Words. (Massachusetts: Harvard University Press, 1962), 6.

[17] Barad, (2007), 140.

[18] Jane Bennett, Vibrant Matter: A Political Ecology of Things. (London: Duke University Press, 2010), 21.

that it is "…a good starting point for thinking beyond the life-matter binary, the dominant organizational principle of adult experience."[19] Moreover, that thing-power represents a disadvantage for it tends to overstate the thinginess or fixed stability of materiality."[20]

In her argument that nonhuman matter, akin to human matter, is active, Bennett draws from Gilles Deleuze and Félix Guattari's concept of the assemblage, a theoretical framework that considers the whole and active "confederation" of matter, to propose that things embody agency. In *A Thousand Plateaus: Capitalism and Schizophrenia*, Deleuze and Guattari famously explain that "[a]n assemblage, in its multiplicity, necessarily acts on semiotic flows, material flows, and social flows simultaneously (independently of any recapitulation that may be made of it in a scientific or theoretical corpus)."[21]

In other words, Deleuze and Guattari's model focuses on the concept of multiplicity, the multiplicity of meaning, the multiplicity of behaviors, and the multiplicity of material entanglements. Furthermore, they note that an assemblage "establishes connections between certain multiplicities drawn from each of these orders, so that a book has no sequel nor the world as its object nor one or several authors as its subject."[22] Adding to Deleuze and Guattari's model, Bennett writes that "[a]ssemblages are [also] ad hoc groupings of diverse elements, of vibrant materials of all sorts. Assemblages are living, throbbing confederations that are able to function despite the persistent presence of energies that confound them from within."[23] In theory, the assemblage, in addition to considering the entire grouping of interacting material sources, also speaks to the dialogical intertwinement that occurs between human and nonhuman matter, or rather breast milk and human participation in *The Lactation Station* [sic].

In chapter three of her book *Vibrant Matter: A Political Ecology of Things*, "Edible Matter," Bennett writes through [sic] her model of the assemblage to understand the entangled relationship between the body and food. Food, in her argument, "…appear[s] as actant inside and alongside intention-forming, morality-(dis)obeying, language-using, reflexivity-wielding, and culture-making human beings, and as an inducer-producer of salient, public effects."[24] With reference to Friedrich Nietzsche and Henry Thoreau, she reflects on the performative act of eating, arguing that upon ingestion, food transforms, by association, into an agent; "[e]ating appears as a series of mutual transformations in which the border between inside and outside becomes blurry: my meal both is and is not mine; you both are and are not what you eat."[25]

By drinking the pasteurized breast milk during Dobkin's performance event, the dividing lines that separate the artist, the mothers, and the spectators also become

---

[19] Ibid. 20.
[20] Idem.
[21] Gilles Deleuze and Félix Guattari, a Thousand Plateaus: Capitalism and Schizophrenia. Translated by Brian Massumi. (Minneapolis: University of Minnesota Press, 1987), 22–23.
[22] Ibid. 23.
[23] Bennett, 23–24.
[24] Ibid. 39.
[25] Ibid. 49.

blurred, transforming the body into an assemblage, and the milk, by association, into performative matter. To quote the philosopher of science Leon Kass, "we do not become the something that we eat; rather the edible gets assimilated to what we are...the edible object is thoroughly transformed by and re-formed into the eater."[26]

In her investigation of nonhuman matter, Bennett exemplifies this interactive and performative nature of "thingness" through the relationship between food as an actant and the act of eating as an assemblage. By linking the transformational act of eating with the agential function of food, she offers a new model that blurs the lines between human and nonhuman matter, in order to highlight the dialogical intertwinement between the body and food.

In Barad's post-humanist reading of material matter, she suggests that nonhuman "things" are not neutral, but inherently inter-active and intra-active. The concept that matter is not singular, nor self-referential, problematizes the neutrality that has traditionally been assigned to materiality—including the materiality of a contemporary studio practice. Through her model of agential realism, a model that understands material agency through its intra-relational exchanges, Barad argues that matter, albeit human or nonhuman, is performative, co-constitutive and materially-discursive; "[m]atter and meaning are not separate elements. They are inextricably fused together, and no event, no matter how energetic, can tear them asunder."[27]

Here, Barad maps an ontological narrative that considers the agential autonomy of matter. In keeping with Jane Bennett's argument that matter is characterized as a "performative" agent that is born from intra-active apparatuses, Barad's task of redefining nonhuman matter aims to question its ethical, metaphysical and ontological intertwinement. In others words, nonhuman matter is inherently discursive and contingent on an entanglement of meaning.

Moreover, Barad understands the performative nature of nonhuman matter in relation to a critical analysis of certain frameworks of poststructuralism that attribute acts of agency to the merely human. For example, feminist cultural theorist Judith Butler specifically does not attribute agency to the body, but instead limits the latter to a discourse of materiality arguing that the body becomes the result of its external material agents.

In the spirit of a material-discursive practice for interpreting the production of meaning, Barad grounds her argument in a scientific deconstruction that reconsiders matter in relation to its intra-active, scientific, and social relationships; "I am not interested in drawing analogies between particles and people, the micro and the macro, the scientific and the social, nature and culture; rather, I am interested in understanding the epistemological and ontological issues that quantum physics forces us to confront, such as the conditions for the possibility of objectivity, the nature of measurement, the nature of nature and meaning making, and the relationship between discursive practices and the material world."[28] In other words, her investigation surrounding the meaning and function of matter asks that [we] move beyond an

---

[26] Leon Kass, The Hungry Soul: Eating and the Perfecting of Our Nature. (Chicago: University of Chicago Press, 1994), 25–26.
[27] Barad, (2007), 3.
[28] Ibid. 24.

aesthetic and representational analysis of its referent, and rather toward an understanding that matter, through intra-activity, becomes a material force that marks the body.

In an ethical debate pertaining to the questions *who or what matters, and when,* Barad refers to feminist sociologist Monica Casper's political interest in dismantling the binaries that distinguish human and nonhuman agency in technoscientific practices. Selfishly admitting that her concerns are rooted in a need to understand "to whom and what in the world [she] is accountable,"[29] Casper draws on the distinctions between female body-as-patient and fetus-as-patient to argue that nonhuman agency should not, in fact, be considered or evaluated in opposition to human agency.

In her own words, "...that actor network theorists, in their principled attribution of agency to human agency is premised on a dichotomous ontological positioning in which [nonhuman] is opposed to human."[30] In the context of an agential realist account, Barad insists that nonhuman matter be considered in relation to its *apparatus*, what she claims is the practice through which the human/nonhuman status of a thing is determined.[31] Yet in the example of Casper's case study of the fetus, the lines that divide the human/nonhuman identity are inextricably blurred, suggesting that perhaps both embody material agency as well as the label of apparatus.

The apparatus, as per Barad, is arguably the root of the performative nature of matter. Loosely defined as a nonhuman (and human) device, practice and action, the apparatus effectively conditions the nature of the practice and is therefore the essence of what generates performativity in relation to material-discursive matter. According to Barad, apparatuses"...are open-ended practices involving specific intra-actions of humans and nonhumans, where the differential constitutions of human and nonhuman designate particular phenomena that are themselves implicated in the dynamics of intra-activity."[32]

In order to fully understand the definition and function of the apparatus, it is also important to know that the apparatus is a contingent, limitless, continuous and ultimately procedural practice of *mattering*. If the apparatus is, as iterated above, an active and procedural assemblage that produces meaning through what Mikhail Bakhtin would call a dialogical exchange, then what is the apparatus in *The Lactation Station* [sic]? Is the apparatus the mother's body? The participant's body? Or is the apparatus a method of performance?

The significance of the apparatus, both in Barad's writing, as well as in my interpretation of material agency vis-à-vis contemporary performance art, is important because it helps to frame how and where matter encounters intra-activity. According to Barad, apparatuses are conceptual spaces for the practice of material-discursivity. These are likened to what Schechner calls the occurrence of transformance; "...apparatuses are *material-discursive practices-causal intra-actions through which matter is iteratively and differentially articulated, reconfiguring the material-discursive field of possibilities and impossibilities in the ongoing dynamics of intra-*

[29] Ibid. 215.
[30] Monica Casper, "Reframing and Grounding Nonhuman Agency: What Makes a Fetus an Agent? American Behavioral Scientist. 37 (6): 839–856, 840.
[31] Barad, (2007), 169.
[32] Ibid. 171.

activity that is agency."[33] In other words, an apparatus is not a tangible object per se, but rather an apparatus translates into a method through which a thing is conceptually transformed into *mattered* matter.

In the context of *The Lactation Station Breast Milk Bar*, the notion of the apparatus parallels the ways in which performance, in this example, becomes a space for material transformance through embodiment. Similar to a materially-discursive space of conceptual transformation, the disciplinary boundaries of performance translate into a metaphorical and political platform on which matter [in this case breast milk] *becomes* through embodied intra-actions. In other words, performance becomes the apparatus while the milk, what Barad would name phenomena, through intra-activity, transforms into a material agent in the event.

Parallel to a scientific explanation that claims that, "...any particular apparatus is always in the process of intra-acting with other apparatuses, and the enfolding of locally stabilized phenomena (which may be traded across laboratories, cultures, or geopolitical spaces only to find themselves differently materializing) into subsequent iterations of particular practices constitutes important shifts in the particular apparatus in question and therefore in the nature of the intra-actions that result in the production of new phenomena, and so on,"[34] breast milk, through the apparatus, begins to exemplify new forms of phenomena. In the example of Casper's writing, the apparatus is embedded within a politically and ethically loaded debate that complicates the associations between the [nonhuman] thing and the [living] apparatus in a scientific context. Dependent on the concept of the apparatus, nonhuman agency becomes, in Butlerian terms *intelligible*, only through an intra-active and subsequently, inter-active connection.

But if the mother's body is the apparatus, as suggested by Barad, how do we identify the fetus? Similar to the complications surrounding breast milk's human/nonhuman nature in *The Lactation Station* [sic], the fetus thus becomes the result of an intra-active entanglement, or rather material agency. Material agency, in essence, cannot be defined through its relationship with the absent presence of human agency. Instead, Casper argues that nonhuman agency is the result of a subjective negotiation between matter and its referent; "...the fetus is not a preexisting object of investigation with inherent properties. Rather the fetus is a phenomenon that is constituted and reconstituted out of historically and culturally specific iterative intra-actions of material-discursive apparatuses of bodily production."[35]

In Dobkin's *The Lactation Station Breast Milk Bar*, milk is a food source produced by the maternal body, and biologically speaking, an animal bi-product that in the performance was pasteurized, packaged, and distributed as a commodity. Framed within a similar binary opposition to that of Casper's debate between the human and nonhuman identity of the fetus, breast milk, in the performance, thus becomes an agent through its intra-active relationship with the performance-turned-apparatus.

---

[33] Ibid. 170.
[34] Barad, (2008), 134–135.
[35] Barad, (2007), 217.

Moreover, if milk becomes matter through a performative exchange, then the argument can be made that it is inherently phenomena because, according to Barad, "…it is through specific intra-actions that phenomena come to matter-in both senses of the word."[36] Here, the word phenomena can be explained as the result of patterns of interactions. More specifically, phenomena, represents a form of performance in which matter engages in an entanglement. Therefore, by blurring the boundaries between performance and the apparatus, it becomes conceptually easier to understand how breast milk and phenomena become entangled. Moreover, it becomes scientifically plausible to parallel milk and phenomena in that both, through intra-activity, become examples of material agency within the space of the laboratory-turned-gallery, or rather gallery-turned-laboratory.

THING-POWER, AND GENDER STUDIES

The concept that an identity is constructed from repeated acts, performative gestures, and semiotic signifiers, according to Judith Butler, complicates the ways in which performance studies scholars understand nonhuman matter in art. Butler's argument suggests that an identity is not innately inherent to gender, more specifically woman, but that an identity is the result of a socio cultural performative exchange.[37] Likened to an aesthetic citation that is constructed through a series of ritualized and repeated acts, Butler explains that; "…the body is only known through its gendered appearance. It would seem imperative to consider the way in which this gendering of the body occurs. My suggestion is that the body becomes its gender through a series of acts which are renewed, revised, and consolidated through time. From a feminist point of view, one might try to reconceive the gendered body as the legacy of sedimented acts rather than a predetermined or foreclosed structure, essence or fact, whether natural, cultural, or linguistic."[38] Focused on acts of *doing* versus the act of *being*, particularly in the context of identity formation, Butler challenges the concept that gender is a pre-existing identity that is pre-scripted and pre-determined arguing, instead, that gender is an open-ended, evolutionary, and flexible identity that remains in constant flux.

In addition to furthering her claim that the body becomes gendered through revised acts of doing in *Bodies That Matter: On the Discursive Limits of "Sex,"* Butler also suggests that the act of doing is paralleled with the idea that gender is the result of a material and constructed citation; "[t]he process of that sedimentation or what we might call *materialization* will be a kind of citationality, the acquisition of being through the citing of power, a citing that establishes an originary [sic] complicity with power in the formation of the 'I.'"[39]

In this context, gender is framed as a material production that is continuously renegotiated in time. However, this concept of construction also lends itself to the

---

[36] Ibid. 140.

[37] Misha Kavka, "Introduction," In Feminist Consequences: Theory for the New Century. Elisabeth Bronfen and Misha Kavka, Ed. (New York: Columbia University Press, 2001), xiv.

[38] Judith Butler, "Performative Acts and Gender Constitution: An Essay in Phenomenology and Feminist Theory," (1988), 523.

[39] Judith Butler (1993), Bodies That Matter: On the Discursive Limits of "Sex." (London and New York: Routledge, 2011), xxiii.

theory that *doing* gender is inherently performative. According to Butler, "...construction is neither a single act nor a causal process initiated by a subject and culminating in a set of fixed effects. Construction not only takes place in time, but is itself a temporal process which operates through the reiteration of norms; sex is both produced and destabilized in the course of this reiteration."[40] In other words, gender becomes a kind of phenomena-performative matter-that remains in constant flux.

In *The Lactation Station* [sic], the concept of construction speaks to the ways in which the artist renegotiates the maternal body/identity of mother construction. By "breastfeeding" other bodies in the gallery, Dobkin re-constitutes her own identity as a mother, as well as the other women's maternal identities. For example, in *Unbearable Weight*, feminist philosopher Susan Bordo argues that a woman becomes a woman when she learns to feed others.

Through feeding practices, Bordo argues, women's bodies perpetuate their femininity, their womanhood, and their maternal agency; "the rules for [the] construction of femininity (and I speak here in a language both symbolic and literal) require that women learn to feed others, not the self, and to construe any desires for self-nurturance and self-feeding as greedy and excessive. Thus, women must develop a totally other-oriented emotional economy. In this economy, the control of female appetite for food is merely the most concrete expression of the general rule governing the construction of femininity: that female hunger-for public power, for independence, for sexual gratification-be contained, and the public space that women be allowed to take up be circumscribed, limited."[41]

The connection between feeding and femininity is a curious correlation in the context of Dobkin's performance, however, because she is, in fact, feeding the audience the same 'food' that other women are feeding their babies: breast milk. However, in keeping with the theme of construction, through the distribution of breast milk, the artist is also constructing her own identity as a mother.

In her writing, Butler asks, "[i]s there a way to link the question of the materiality of the body to the performativity of gender?"[42] More specifically, is embodiment performative? The short answer is yes. The body, according to Butler, is an autonomous being whose identity is intelligible. But more important is the concept that the body *does* the body, resulting in an inevitable form of temporary and ever-changing embodiment; "...the body is not merely matter but a continual and incessant *materializing* of possibilities. One is not simply a body, but, in some very key sense, one does one's body and, indeed, one does one's body differently from one's contemporaries and from one's embodied predecessors and successors as well."[43]

In other words, materials become material manifestations of their procedural relationships with other *things*. For example, in *The Lactation Station Breast Milk Bar*, breast milk extends beyond a signifier for the maternal body. Rather, it manifests into a material agent [phenomena] whose performative nature remains in constant flux, thus continually reinventing itself vis-à-vis the human body. The fact that Dobkin

---

[40] Ibid. xix.
[41] Susan Bordo, Unbearable Weight, (Berkeley: California University Press, 1993), 171.
[42] Butler, (1993), xi.
[43] Butler, (1988), 521.

uses something we ingest in our own materializing bodies leads [us] to the idea that the materialization of food itself is also an unstable one, similar to and actually sometimes [sic], aligned with gender as a performative act.

Parallel to the concept that milk, in Dobkin's performance, *does* the body is the notion that food *does* one's gender in the field of gastronomical literature. One of the earliest distinctions between gender and food writing is rooted in the claim that men were authors of gastronomy while women were authors of cookbooks. During a time when women wrote cookbooks and men were scholars of gastronomy, Alice B. Toklas, Gertrude Stein's lover and long-time partner, challenged the gender politics inherent within what is today labeled food studies. Curious about the influence of food on gender, sexuality and society, hers was, in theory and practice, an argument that food is in essence performative.[44]

In *Aesthetic Pleasure in Twentieth-Century Women's Food Writing: The Innovative Appetites of M.F.K. Fisher, Alice B. Toklas, and Elizabeth David*, Alice L. McLean maps a social and political history of the evolution of gastronomical literature through a feminist lens. With reference to Elizabeth David's understanding and appropriation of food [writing], McLean notes that through food, women could begin to understand themselves as social and sexual bodies; "…food encouraged a sensory engagement with her environment and a physical receptivity toward pleasure that engendered her creative aesthetic."[45]

Furthermore, according to McLean, "…David educated her readers to approach food as more than just an end in itself, to understand eating and cooking as means of self-construction as well as self-expression."[46] Although through a different medium, Dobkin too is channeling Toklas' same revolutionary ambition to explore the function of food in relation to sexuality, and gender roles in performance art.

Like her predecessor, Dobkin is a self-identified lesbian working to dismantle stereotypes. Through the act of sharing breast milk in *The Lactation Station Breast Milk Bar*, however, hers is also a debate between homosexuality and motherhood. Or rather, is the artist's identity being constructed, and perpetuated, through her ability, or truthfully inability, to produce breast milk? Moreover, does this mean that a lesbian can biologically also be a mother?

In the performance, the act of undoing the body is physically and metaphorically exemplified by Dobkin, who literally undoes the maternal body by collecting its milk

---

[44] Alice B. Toklas was an early rebel in the field of gastronomic literature. A self-identified lesbian, and queer modern epicure, Toklas consistently blurred the gendered lines between scholarly writing, and domestic food writing by dissolving the boundaries between so-called cookbook writing and gastronomical writing. For example, in addition to inserting recipes into her narrative, she freely moved between the personal and the public to create what today would be called a foodie travelogue. By challenging the power of the male voice in this field, Toklas was not only redefining the ways in which women were involved with gastronomy, but more importantly she was challenging the performative relationship between food, gender and sexuality in the everyday. ."..Toklas figures herself as a queer modern epicure-equally at ease in the home kitchen as in the most elite restaurants. Her self-presentation calls into question and reconfigures the nineteenth and early twentieth-century ideologies that defined gastronomy and gastronomic tourism as male pursuits and domestic cookery as feminine endeavor." Alice L. McLean, Aesthetic Pleasure in Twentieth-Century Women's Food Writing:The Innovative Appetites of M.F.K Fisher, Alice B. Toklas, and Elizabeth David. (London and New York: Routledge, 2012), 93.

[45] Ibid. 1.

[46] Ibid. 142.

and sharing it. In theory, by serving donated breast milk, the artist transforms her role as the performer into that of a facilitator and participant. However, these acts also problematize the concept of performativity by blurring the material lines between human and nonhuman matter. As an active and participatory agent in this piece, milk becomes the performer in the gallery through its new role as a transformative agent. In keeping with Butler's argument that gender, through the act of doing, becomes performative, then the milk, by comparison, through its ability to blur the roles between performer and participant, also becomes performative matter.

The argument that nonhuman matter *matters*, according to Barad, supports the ongoing theory that milk, in this inquiry, is not discursive, nor pre-existent, but rather performative through intra-activity. Critical of Butler's claim that matter is only materialized to produce an *identity*, Barad argues that matter is not only a material thing, but that it is an active, and transformative phenomena that continually reproduces the boundaries and conditions of being;[47] "...Butler's theory ultimately reinscribes matter as a passive product of discursive practices rather than as an active agent participating in the very process of materialization." [48] In other words, nonhuman matter, in the realm of gender studies, is a neutral material that conditions the aesthetics of gender, of an identity, and of sexuality. Yet, matter, according to Barad is also a transformative entity that is never neutral, nor limited to representation.

More problematic than Butler's argument that only the human body is representative of matter are the ways in which she understands gender through its material surface; "[p]erhaps the most crucial limitation of Butler's theory of materiality is that it is limited to an account of the materialization of human bodies (or, more accurately, to the construction of the surface of the human body, which most certainly is not all there is to human bodies)."[49] In the context of post-humanist performativity and the argument that materials are performative, Butler's writing limits the debate that nonhuman materials are in theory and practice agential.

The relationship between matter and breast milk, in *The Lactation Station* [sic], is equally complicated when considered through a Butlerian lens because Butler's model neglects to account for the transformative processes that make milk edible. Breast milk is originally a source of food for a baby produced by a mother's body. According to Western traditions, it is not intended to be pasteurized for consumption like the milk produced by animals. In comparison, cow, goat, and sheep's milk undergoes a process of pasteurization in which it is heated in order to kill any potential bacteria.

Yet, breast milk, which is not intended for the adult body, is also not meant for pasteurization. In addition to providing digestive enzymes, protein, and vitamins to newborn babies, the act of breastfeeding also benefits the mother's body by reducing the risks of post-partum bleeding and post-partum depression. But traditionally, breast milk is not a food source intended for the consumption of the adult body in that its ingredients are biologically specific for its intended consumer—a baby.

In the context of the argument that materials are performative in contemporary art, breast milk becomes a curious example of material agency in that it is both a live

---

[47] Barad, (2007), 150.
[48] Ibid. 151.
[49] Ibid. 209.

human bi-product that is inherently agential, as well as a material that, in Dobkin's performance, becomes a performative subject through distribution and ingestion. Distinguished by taste, color, and even name, the so-called lead actor in the gallery is never the same, or neutral.

Instead, breast milk's ever-changing nature suggests that it is alive and active through biological, cultural, and social transformance. Influenced by factors such as a mother's age, their diet, the age and gender of the baby, as well as the materialization of the spectator-turned-participant, each "milk-tail" [sic] had a unique taste. Thus, if the milk's "identity" remains active after pasteurization, then arguably so does its status as a performative material [in art].

Through *The Lactation Station Breast Milk Bar*, the problematic [sic] surrounding the performativity of nonhuman materials becomes embedded within a larger debate surrounding the questions: who or what matters in contemporary performance art? Moreover, the debate pertaining to performative agency lends itself to a more complicated inquiry into the ways in which post humanist performativity accounts for the inherent material agency of the "stuff of a studio practice."

Although human through its (biological) relationship to the body, breast milk, in the context of this event, becomes more than a substance produced by a mother's body. Milk, in this example, transforms into an agent, an actant, a producer and a participant. [50] In other words, milk, through its intra-active relationship with performance and its consumer, suggests that a material, which is both active and socio-cultural can be seen as performative phenomena [matter].

BIBLIOGRAPHY

Austin, John L. *How To Do Things With Words.* (Massachusetts: Harvard University Press, 1962).

Bakhtin, Mikhail. *Problems of Dostoevsky's Poetics.* Translated by Caryl Emerson. (London and Minneapolis: University of Minnesota Press, 1984).

————"Toward a Methodology for the Human Sciences." 1974.

Barad, Karen. Meeting the Universe Halfway: Quantum Physics and the Entanglement of Matter and Meaning. (London: Duke University Press, 2007).

————"Post humanist Performativity: Toward an Understanding of How Matter Came to Matter." In *Signs: Journal of Women in Culture and Society.* (Chicago: University of Chicago Press. 2003).

Barthes, Roland. *Camera Lucida: Reflections on Photography.* Translated by Richard Howard. (New York: Hill and Wang, 1981).

---

[50] Actants, according to Bruno Latour, represent a "source of action; an actant can be human or not, or, most likely, a combination of both...as something that acts or to which activity is granted by others." Bruno Latour, "On Actor-Network Theory:A Few Clarifications." Soziale Welt: 47, no. 4, 1996, 369–381.

————*Mythologies*. Paris: Editions du Seuil, 1957; Translated by Annette Lavers, (New York: Hill and Wang, 1972).

————The Responsibility of Forms: Critical Essays on Music, Art, and Representation. (Berkeley: University of California Press, 1991).

Bennett, Jane. *Vibrant Matter: A Political Ecology of Things.* (London: Duke University Press, 2010).

Bishop, Claire. Artificial Hells: Participatory Art and the Politics of Spectatorship. (London and New York:Verso Books, 2012).

————Installation Art: A Critical History. (New York: Routledge, 2005).

————*Participation*. (London: Whitechapel; Cambridge: MIT Press, 2006).

Bordo, Susan. *Unbearable Weight.* (Berkeley: California University Press, 1993).

Braidotti, Rosi. Nomadic Subjects: Embodiment and Sexual Difference in Contemporary Feminist Theory. (New York: Columbia University Press, 1994).

Butler, Judith. *Bodies That Matter:On the Discursive Limits of "Sex."* (London and New York: Routledge, 1993, 2011).

———— *Frames of War: When Is Life Grievable?* (London and New York: Verso, 2010).

———— *Gender Trouble.* (New York and London: Routledge, 1990).

———— "Performative Acts and Gender Constitution: An Essay in Phenomenology and Feminist Theory," 1988.

Butler—Kisber, Lynn. Qualitative Inquiry: Thematic, Narrative and Arts—Informed Perspectives. (London: SAGE Publications, 2010).

Casper, Monica. "Reframing and Grounding Nonhuman Agency: What Makes a Fetus an Agent? *American Behavioral Scientist.* 37 (6): 839–856.

Chandler, John, and Lucy Lippard. "The Dematerialization of Art." *Art International*, Vol. 12, no. 2, February 1968: 31–32.

Deleuze, Gilles, and Félix Guattari. *A Thousand Plateaus: Capitalism and Schizophrenia.* Translated by Brian Massumi. (Minneapolis: University of Minnesota Press, 1987).

Deutsche, Rosalyn. *Evictions: Art and Spatial Politics.* (Cambridge and London: The MIT Press, 1998).

———— "Public Art and Its Uses." In *Critical Issues in Public Art, Content, Context and Controversy.* Harriet Senie, and Sally Webster. Ed. (New York: Icon Editions, 1992).

——— "The Question of Public Space" conference paper, *The Photography Institute*, 1998.

Dewey, John. *Art as Experience*. (New York:Minton, Balch and Company, 1934).

Drobnick, Jim and Jennifer Fisher. "MUSEOPATHY." In *MUSEOPATHY*. (Kingston: Agnes Etherington Centre, Queen's University in association with DisplayCult, 2001),

Fischer—Lichte, Erika. *The Transformative Power of Performance: A New Aesthetics*. Translated by Saskya Iris Jain. (London and New York: Routledge Press, 2008).

Fried, Michael. *Art and Objecthood: Essays and Reviews*. (Chicago and London: The University of Chicago Press, 1998).

Haraway, Donna J. "Compoundings" *Sensorium: Embodied Experience, Technology, and Contemporary Art*. Jones, Caroline A., Bill Arning. Eds. (Cambridge: MIT Press: MIT List Visual Arts Center, 2006).

——— Simians, Cyborgs and Women: The Reinvention of Nature. (New York: Routledge, 1991).

——— The Companion Species Manifesto: Dogs, People, and Significant Otherness. (Chicago: Prickly Paradigm, 2003).

——— "The Promises of Monsters: A Regenerative Politics of Inappropriate/d Others." In *Cultural Studies*. Lawrence Grossberg, Cary Nelson and Paula Treichler. Ed. (London and New York: Routledge, 1992) 295–337.

——— *When Species Meet*. (Minneapolis and London: University of Minnesota Press, 2008).

Herzig, Rebecca. "On Performance, Productivity and Vocabularies of Motive in Recent Studies of Science." In *Feminist Theory* 2004), 5.

Howes, David. "Charting the Sensorial Revolution." *Sense and Society*. 1, no. 1, 2006.

———"Hearing Scents, Tasting Sights: Toward a Cross—Cultural Multimodal Theory of Aesthetics." In *Art and the Senses*. Francesca Bacci, David Melcher. Ed. (Oxford: Oxford University Press, 2011).

———Sensual Relations: Engaging the Senses in Culture and Social Theory. (Ann Arbor: The University of Michigan Press, 2006).

Jones, Amelia. *Body Art: Performing the Subject*. (London and Minneapolis: University of Minnesota Press, 1998).

Jones, Amelia, and Adrian Heathfield. *Perform, Repeat, Record: Live Art in History*. (Bristol and Chicago: Intellect, 2012).

Jones, Amelia, and Andrew Stephenson. Ed. *Performing the Body/Performing the Text*. (London and New York: Routledge, 1999).

Jones, Caroline A., Bill Arning. *Sensorium: Embodied Experience, Technology, and Contemporary Art*. (Cambridge: MIT Press: MIT List Visual Arts Center, 2006).

Kass, Leon. *The Hungry Soul: Eating and the Perfecting of Our Nature*. (Chicago: University of Chicago Press, 1994).

Kavka, Misha. "Introduction," In *Feminist Consequences: Theory for the New Century*. Elisabeth Bronfen and Misha Kavka, Ed. (New York: Columbia University Press, 2001).

Latour, Bruno. "On Actor—Network Theory: A Few Clarifications." Soziale Welt: 47, no. 4, 1996.

———Reassembling the Social: Introduction to Actor Network Theory. (London: Oxford University Press, 2005).

Lippard, Lucy. *From the Center: Feminist Essays on Women's Art*. (New York: E.P. Dutton, 1976).

———Overlay: Contemporary Art and the Art of Prehistory. (New York: Pantheon, 1983).

———The Lure of the Local: Senses of Place in a Multicultural Society. (New York: New Press, 1997).

McLean, Alice L. Aesthetic Pleasure in Twentieth-Century Women's Food Writing: The Innovative Appetites of M.F.K Fisher, Alice B. Toklas, and Elizabeth David. (London and New York: Routledge, 2012).

Melrose, Susan. "Bodies without Bodies." *Performance and Technology: Practices of Virtual Embodiment and Interactivity*. Susan Broadhurst and Josephine Machon. Ed. (New York: Palgrave Macmillan, 2006).

Miller, J. Hillis. "Performativity as Performance/Performativity as Speech Act: Derrida's Special Theory of Performativity." *South Atlantic Quarterly*, 106: 2, Spring 2007.

Myers, Natasha. "Pedagogy and Performativity: Rendering Lives in Science in the Documentary *Naturally Obsessed: The Making of a Scientist.' Isis:* Focus Section on Performing Science." 101 (4): 817–828, 2010.

Nochlin, Linda. "Why Have There Been No Great Women Artists?" *Art News*, January 1971; reprinted in *Women, Art and Power and Other Essays*. (New York: Harper & Row, 1988).

Noland, Carrie. *Agency and Embodiment: Performing Gestures/Producing Culture*. (London and Massachusetts: Harvard University Press, 2009).

Nygard, Travis. "Food and Art" in Albala, Ken. Ed. *Routledge International Handbook of Food Studies*. (London and New York: Routledge, 2013).

Pickering, Andrew. "After Dualism." *Challenges to Dominant Modes of Knowledge: Dualism*, Sponsored by the Gulbenkian Foundation. SUNY Binghamton, November 3–4, 2006.

————"The Mangle of Practice: Agency and Emergence in the Sociology of Science." In *The Science Studies Reader*. Mario Biagoli, Ed. (New York: Routledge, 1999).

Pollock, Griselda. Differencing the Canon: Feminist Desire and the Writing of Art's Histories. (London and New York: Routledge, 1999).

Reeve, Charles. "The Kindness of Human Milk: Jess Dobkin's *Lactation Station Breast Milk Bar*." *Gastronomica*, winter 2009: 70.

Schechner, Richard. *Performance Theory*. (London and New York: Routledge, 1988).

Schimmel, Paul. *Out of Actions: Between Performance and the Object, 1949–1979*. Los Angeles: The Museum of Contemporary Art: Thames and Hudson, 1998

Turner, Victor. *From Ritual to Theater: The Human Seriousness of Play*. (New York: PAJ Publications, 1982).

CHAPTER 9

The Rasa of Immersive and Participatory Theatre

Erin Mee

"Unwrap your chocolate, place it on your tongue, close your eyes, and let your tongue choreograph the dance of chocolate,' instructed Alice B. Toklas in This Is Not A Theatre Company's *A Serious Banquet*. Music wafted over the dinner guests as they created a private dance in the mouth. By giving time-space to the sensoria, engaging partakers as co-creators of the event, and focusing on affect, immersive and participatory productions such as *A Serious Banquet* are inherently *rasic*.

The Sanskrit term *"rasa"* has been variously translated as juice, flavor, extract, and essence. In the context of performance theory, it is the "aesthetic flavor or sentiment" *tasted* in and through performance. *The Natyasastra*, the Sanskrit aesthetic treatise attributed to Bharata, notes that when foods and spices are mixed together in different ways, they create different tastes; similarly, the mixing of different basic emotions arising from different situations, when expressed through the performer—or, in the case of immersive and participatory theatre, through the smell of garlic, the taste of chocolate, or the gentle touch of a hand—gives rise to an *emotional* experience or "taste" in the partaker, which is rasa (Bharata 55, emphasis mine).

In fact, rasa is more than taste, it is pleasure: "Persons who eat prepared food mixed with different condiments and sauces, etc., if they are sensitive, enjoy the different tastes and then feel pleasure (or satisfaction); likewise, sensitive spectators [...] feel pleasure" (Bharata 55). Rasa is, as the tenth-century aesthetic theorist Abhinavagupta, who commented extensively on *The Natyasastra*, puts it, an *"act of relishing"* (in Deshpande, emphasis mine). For Abhinavagupta, rasa is not a gift bestowed upon a passive spectator, but an attainment, an accomplishment—someone who wants to experience rasa has to be an active participant in the work. The partaker has to interact: like a meal, rasa exists neither in the artwork (the food) nor in the partaker, but in their *interaction*. It is a *shared* experience, one that has been described as "the *process* of aesthetic perception itself" (Deutsch 1981: 215, emphasis mine), which means rasa exists only *when* and *as* it is experienced. Thus rasa posits the interactive audience as participant and partaker—and co-creator—of the event. Rasa is active, sensorial, experiential, and embodied. It is, then, a theory of aesthetic immersion and participation. As such, it is the best way to understand and describe the aesthetic underpinnings of immersive and participatory theatre.

A Serious Banquet (Judson Church and New York Theatre Workshop, 2014) was a cubist dinner structured around the party Pablo Picasso threw for the painter Henri

Rousseau in 1908 Paris. If cubism is the opportunity to see something from multiple angles and perspectives at once, this piece asked: what would a cubist *play* be? What would a cubist *experience* be? What would a cubist dinner party be? What would a cubist world view be? We live in a world where the algorithms in our news feeds and on Facebook structure our reading to give us more of what we "like." We are, according to social scientists, increasingly surrounded by people who think the way we do and are always already in agreement with us. In other words, we are in danger of not being challenged by "other" perspectives, of living in an echo chamber of our own ideas. *A Serious Banquet* challenged singular perspectives in many ways, most obviously in that key scenes were repeated from different emotional and visual perspectives so audiences could experience the same scene from many "angles"—a theatrical version of cubism. *A Serious Banquet* invited audiences to step out of the various forms of cognitive closure we all experience, to see situations (and characters) from several angles at once, and thus to practice complex seeing.

Partakers of *A Serious Banquet* were welcomed into the world of the play by Picasso's overly-perfumed mistress Fernande Olivier. They were asked to deliver a rose to Gertrude Stein—which gave them a task to perform; they were invited to converse with a guitar programmed to respond to speech with music; they were asked to answer the phone, which recited Guillaume Apollinaire poems; they were encouraged to sign the birthday card for Rousseau; they were invited to listen to a still life (a bottle and vase that had a scene with each other); they were chosen to participate in a recitation/demonstration of Gertrude Stein's continuous present; they were invited to sit in a two-dimensional painting of a chair—which turned out to be an actual three-dimensional chair; they were given wine and/or water at a table that had a special skillet designed to fill the room with the smell of food; they were invited to view Picasso's "Les Demoiselles D'Avignon" recreated with live bodies; and they were asked to introduce Apollinaire (played by a glass of absinthe containing a speaker) to other guests. In this way, as both performer and partaker, they co-created the event. Their actions and experiences became an integral and essential part of the evening; in fact, they became what Gareth White calls "the work's aesthetic material" (White 2013: 9–10). One audience member said that the event "made [her] think of the experience of creation as a liminal space between the individual experience and decisions of the artist [which is rasa]…but at the same time art creation as a collective experience in which we shared a space and a moment [which is also rasa]" (Audience A).

After all the guests had arrived, they had an opportunity to experience "salon" moments—one-on-one interactions with various characters. Georges Braque took a single audience member to the corner bodega to get more ice while discussing art and cubism; Max Jacob enlisted an audience member's help in creating a poem; Picasso (played by a woman in this production) invited three audience members to paint on miniature canvases with nail polish and to discuss art. Alice Toklas took one audience member outside for a cigarette, and told them how she arrived in Paris. One audience member wrote: "a highlight of my evening was sitting and having a conversation with 'Gertrude Stein' and then having her paint a word portrait of me—an impromptu improvisation part poem, part song, it was a moment that continues to resonate with me and makes me long for great parties where everyone feels they can let go and express themselves creatively" (Audience B). Even moments that were "scripted," were tailored to the specific inter-actions between actor-character and partaker.

Many of the immersive and participatory performances in New York, Barcelona, and London—including *Then She Fell, Queen of the Night, Symposium, Bar Play, Alice in London, Play/Date, Tony 'n' Tina's Wedding, Versailles 2015, A Serious Banquet, Three Sisters*, all the work of Teatro de los Sentidos, and most of the work done by Woodshed Collective, to name just a few examples—include food and/or drink. In most cases, the food and drink is not just an attempt to lower inhibitions (although it can serve that function too). In most cases, it is an attempt to create a multi-sensory, multimodal, semi-synaesthetic, embodied engagement. Interestingly, drinking and eating in a production literalizes Bharata's central metaphor for rasa.

After the salon moments, everyone sat down to dinner. They drew dinner plates on a paper tablecloth, and three-dimensional food was served on their two-dimensional plates. During dinner, characters offered their birthday gifts to Rousseau in the form of a sculpture made of audience members (Picasso); a silent dance by Ida Rubenstein; a cabaret song by the Demoiselles D'Avignon; and poetry by Max Jacob, Andre Salmon, and Gertrude Stein. The dance of chocolate was one of the highlights of the evening for many partakers. As one critic put it:

> Celebration is a sensorial experience. As is art. This evening is an experience, a way to discover cubist art from other vantage points, through other senses. I was, at one point, asked to put a piece of chocolate in my mouth, and then, with my tongue, to make it dance. I love chocolate, and I love savoring food and drink, but to make it dance made it something so much more. And I was asked to discuss Picasso's latest painting, and to draw myself my dinner plate, and…
>
> And that's it too: there was an invitation here. Often I was asked to help create. My friend got to make miniature paintings while I listened for what I might find within a conversation between a vase and a bottle (of which I didn't realize later would be a gift I was to give). I was handed markers, and so convinced a painting to draw with me. I was invited to an evening of joy.
>
> This "play" isn't a play at all. It is an invitation to experience celebration. Yes, it is about art and history, but these things were not handed to me in a dusty book, or put upon a stage where it could judge me for not knowing enough. I was allowed instead to play and grapple with the work, not as a spectator but as a creator myself—not from the outside peering in, but from within itself (McConnell 2014).

A situation that privileges the smell of garlic and rosemary, the touch of other people, and the taste of chocolate—the multisensory world of immersive and participatory theatre—privileges the feeling body. Not only did the partakers' actions and experiences become "the work's aesthetic material" (White 2013:9–10), but their emotional responses shaped and became the event: "The feeling body," as Erin

Hurley claims, is "the vehicle for [immersive and participatory] theatre's images and execution. The feeling body is both the basis and the means of theatre" (2010:36).

The feeling body is an affected and affecting body. Affect can be "found in those intensities that pass body to body [...] in those resonances that circulate" about and between bodies. These are also the affective interactions in which rasa can be found. Both affect and rasa "arise in the midst of in-between-ness [and] in the capacities to act and be acted upon." If "the capacity of a body is never defined by a body alone, but by [...] the context of its force-relations," and "affect is integral to a body's perpetual becoming," (Gregg and Seigworth 2010: Kindle locations 50, 51, 72) then rasa is a mechanism for privileging the constant becoming of the affected body; which positions immersive and participatory theatre as forces of affective change. The constant becoming of affected and affecting bodies interacting in the room allows for a fluid subjectivity that is "assembled and re-assembled through" encounters with others (and with different situations) during the course of the evening (White 2013:24).

In *Poetics*, Aristotle speaks of the role of music, as experienced in certain religious rites, in the treatment of emotional people (8.7.1342a 4–15). "For any emotional excitement that affects some souls strongly also occurs to a lesser or greater degree in everyone—pity, fear, or again religious ecstasy [*enthousiasmos*]. There are some people who are particularly susceptible to this latter form of excitement and we see them, once they have made use of the most rousing melodies, put back on their feet again as a result of the sacred melodies just as if they had obtained medical treatment and katharsis. People predisposed to feeling pity or fear, or to emotions generally, necessarily undergo the same experience, as do others to the extent that they share in each of these emotions, and for all a certain katharsis and alleviation accompanied by pleasure" (in Hall forthcoming).

AS NOTED CLASSICIST EDITH HALL POINTS OUT:

This discussion constitutes crucial evidence for the acknowledged power possessed by some special sacred melodies in helping ancient Greeks handle extreme emotions [...] Here Aristotle is certainly talking about emotional katharsis. Emotions pre-exist in people, but they can be stimulated by an external force in a way that makes them susceptible to katharsis. An externally applied 'treatment' (music [or theatre]) actually creates a homeopathic response within the listeners [spectators], in that the arousal of a strong emotion to which they are predisposed leads to a lessening of the grip which that emotion has on them. (Hall forthcoming).

Katharsis is about purging excess emotion. In contradistinction, rasa is about celebrating or relishing emotion. The goal is affect rather than effect. Katharsis demands a linear dramaturgical structure that builds to an ultimate release of tension or excess emotion in the form of a climax, followed by a denouement. A leads to B, which builds to C, which builds to D, and so on until the climax is reached. In contradistinction, rasa requires a nonlinear, flexible dramaturgical structure that allows the partaker to linger in/with particular moments and to "wander around" exploring numerous sensorial stimuli which give rise to emotions that can be savored.

To return to the metaphor of food: an *amuse bouche* is an experience to relish in and of itself; it is not a prerequisite for the appetizer. Nor is the appetizer a prerequisite for the main course. Although my mother considered vegetables to be a prerequisite for dessert, dessert was never the main "goal" of a meal, and we still felt as though we had eaten if we didn't have dessert. A meal has things that come before and things that come after, and certain tastes compliment or interact with each other, but D does not depend on C or B or A: you can still understand and appreciate a main course if you have not had an appetizer.

Immersive and participatory productions consciously create nonlinear structures to give the audience opportunities to relish an environment, a scene, a character, a prop, a smell, a texture, a taste, and/or a sound, in their own way and in their own time. A non-linear structure allowed audiences to relish Emily Dickinson in Theater Plastique's *Emily Dickinson: Outer Space* (Bushwick Starr, 2014) a 54-hour continuous celebration of her work. Audiences could come for a few minutes, stay for the entire fifty-four hours, or come and go as they wished. They could sit around and watch the action; they could dance by themselves, with each other, and/or with cast members; they could eat and/or drink; they could bring a Dickinson poem and have cast members set it to music and sing it on the spot; they could recite a Dickinson poem themselves; they could take a break from the "action" and nap in the onstage "igloo" (or, as some apparently did, have sex in the igloo). Part rave, part slumber party, part cabaret, part rehearsal (depending on what time of day or night you went), the idea was to spend as many hours as you could relishing Dickinson's beautiful language and imagery. The event had no discernible structure, but functioned as a time-space where anyone who loved Dickinson could hang out and party with other people who loved Dickinson. Had it had a structure, we might not have been able to follow our moment-to-moment instincts and collectively fête Dickinson with our sweat, our voices, our dream-like, fatigue-induced excitement, and our interactions with others who love her work.

Aristotle's aesthetic theory of katharsis is based on the notion of seeing (*teatron*, place of seeing), which requires distance (to get perspective). Rasa requires an embodied and internalized process of tasting, touching, and entering into (see Schechner 2015). Highly Impractical Theatre's *Three Sisters* (A House in Brooklyn, 2014) offered several ways to experience Irina's birthday party. I went once as a serf, helping Anfisa pour "vodka" for the guests and serve food to the aristocrats at table. I went a second time as an aristocrat and, because I was allowed to wander around upstairs, saw scenes I had literally not seen the first time; sat in places I did not sit the first time (I never sat as a serf); and had a very different experience of Irina's party—I felt I had actually been invited. I have seen many productions of *Three Sisters*, but this is the first one that asked me to think so deeply about the class divisions in Chekhov's plays because I had to experience them. My role dictated my status, which in turn dictated my behavior, the spaces I inhabited, the information I was privy to, what I ate and drank (or didn't), whom I spoke to, and how I viewed the action around me. Admittedly, I had to re-read the play before I went—I would have been lost without brushing up on the plot and characters because I did not see "the whole play,"

I saw the parts of it my character had access to. I was not an "objective observer." I entered the world of the play.

One of my students described his experience with the character Masha:

> She signaled that I should follow her after we locked eyes. Sirens sounded, and I [...] trailed her through a maze of hallways and staircases that seemed to muffle her troubled life. Up a final staircase, and we were safe, alone. I bent my knees and slid next to a small collection of curios that sat on the landing. She gazed at these love notes, pictures, and candles; I felt as if I had access to her memories. She was silent. The sounds of the house had faded away, and after a few long moments, my guide held out her hand. "Masha," she said. "Sam," I said. "Look," and she pointed to the open skylight that I hadn't noticed above my head. A breeze blew through, and it seemed as if the turmoil going on below us had dematerialized. Masha was quiet as she looked at the sky, and I sensed her deep sadness as voices called out her name from below, and she led me back downstairs [...] In my time with Masha, I was allowed to live with her in a private moment of fear and confusion. I empathized with her. I understood her [...] I was implicated in her personal drama, and lost my ability to remain [critically] removed from the play. (Silbiger 2014).

My student was bothered by the fact that he lost what he referred to as his "objectivity" and his "ability to remain [critically] removed from the play." But losing one's objectivity is in fact the point. Immersive and participatory theatre reveals the falseness in the very idea of objectivity (which is always already subjective), and revels in partial perceptions: unlike the proscenium where the spectator believes she can see everything, immersive and participatory theatre are set up in such a way that the partaker cannot possibly see everything—and is aware of that. The partial view is celebrated. Objectivity is not the point. Subjectivity, in all aspects, is.

Jacques Ranciere claims that the audience-performance relationship in conventional proscenium theatre is designed to bring audiences into "our" (playwrights, directors, actors, designers, dramaturgs) superior understanding (see Ranciere 2009). The politics of a rasic experience are quite different: instead of having two distinct groups—one acting and another acted upon—everyone in participatory performance has agency to co-create the event, to make their own meaning, and to have their experiences and understandings matter. Production and reception are intertwined (see Fischer-Lichte 2008).

"What do you see?" The psychologist points at an inkblot on the gallery wall and audience members shout out: "a butterfly!" "a vagina!" "an extraterrestrial!" This is one of twenty-eight scenes in This Is Not A Theatre Company's *Readymade Cabaret* (Judson Church, 2015). Other scenes include a dance titled "We Make Up Stories To Hide The Fact That Beneath Our Feet Lies An Abyss of Meaninglessness" which consists of one actor walking back and forth in a straight line while another actor walks in a circle; and a scene titled "Conclusions," in which Amy says: "And I guess that's the hardest part of life, in general. Meaninglessness. Randomness. Chaos. Sometimes, things just happen." This Is Not A Theatre Company's *Readymade*

Cabaret, based on Marcel Duchamp's notion of readymade art and the philosophies of Dada as practiced by Duchamp and Tristan Tzara, takes place in a "gallery" in the basement of Judson Church in New York City occupied by readymade artwork lining the walls. Performers are posed in the space as if they too are readymades. One critic said that as audience members filed in, helped to construct a Dada poem, added a noise-making object to the musical instrument titled With Hidden Noise, and looked at the artwork, she realized "This was no ordinary museum. The space was a sort of incubator, eliciting a mode of audience hyper-attention: of placing every object, human, and their interactions under the scrutiny of complete visibility that is fluorescent lighting" (Lee 2015). A gong sounds, and the performers direct our attention to a pillar on which there are twenty-eight scene titles, including: "Amy Does Believe in Fate," "Amy Doesn't Believe in Fate," "Lab Rats," and "What Richard Wiseman Has to Say About Luck." Two scenes titled "An End" and "Another End" share the bottom slot. An audience member is invited to roll a die. The number on the die dictates which scene will be performed. Twenty of the twenty-eight scenes about control, fate, free will, and chance are performed. The narrative scenes are written so that a random selection of scenes will create recurring characters and plotlines that the audience can follow—or create. For example, Amy and Peter are in a relationship; Amy works for Dr. Burton conducting an experiment with rats to determine which parts of the brain are involved in our need to make meaning; a Professor lectures his class on "Why The Greeks Had It So Easy" (because they believed in fate); and another Professor discusses the brain's tendency to make meaning. Scenes also include an aleatory composition, a version of John Cage's 4:33, opportunities to stand and look at various sculptures and installations, and #TweetDances—one-minute improvised dances prompted by audience tweets set to music chosen by the shuffle function on the stage manager's iPad. Because the scenes that are performed and the order in which they are performed literally depend on the roll of the dice, the audience sees one of over a million possible plays in any given performance.

Duchamp's readymades are known as artworks that question the definition and role of art: is art something "original" "created" by an artist; an extant object collaged or chosen by an artist; or does something become a piece of art when it is (re)contextualized or viewed as art—in which case, does the viewer "create" the art by seeing something as art? *Readymade Cabaret* is a participatory production: it is one of many productions that examines the role of the audience created not only by This Is Not A Theatre Company, but by Gob Squad, Analogue, Third Rail Productions, Action Hero, Rimini Protokoll, Search Party, Woodshed Collective, Blast Theory, Rotozaza, and Punchdrunk. However, *Readymade Cabaret* is perhaps more directly connected to performance art pieces such as Yoko Ono's *Cut Piece*, Fusco and Gomez-Pena's *Couple In A Cage*, and Marina Abramovic's piece in which she laid seventy-two items out on a table and invited the audience to use them on her as they saw fit. In these pieces, the audience understands—or learns—that their instincts, desires, actions, and reactions are what the piece is about. The audience is not the medium; the way they participate is the message.

How did audiences make their way through *Readymade Cabaret*? One participant used Tzara's instructions for creating a Dada poem (which the audience did, and the reading of the poem was one of the 28 possible scenes) as a "roadmap:"

Take a newspaper.

Take some scissors.

Choose from this paper an article of the length you want to make your poem.

Cut out the article.

Next carefully cut out each of the words that make up this article and put them all in a bag.

Shake gently.

Next take out each cutting one after the other.

Copy conscientiously in the order in which they left the bag.

The poem will resemble you.

And there you are—an infinitely original author of charming sensibility, even though unappreciated by the vulgar herd.

She decided that each scene was like a word in the Dada poem, and that the way she put them together resembled her. Another audience member wrote: "I started thinking about the more traditionally verbal 'playlets' as structural markers and that all of them were about the same characters having different interactions at different points in time, which together created a narrative about a relationship that was evolving in time and space. This helped pace and shape the overall piece for me. But I would also say that that sort of structuring wasn't really necessary. The piece was enjoyable as a random assemblage in its own right." Yet another wrote: "I'm the kind of idle walker that kind of likes to get lost and find my way "back" again (Venice is great for that) because wherever I am, I'm in place. That's the way I traveled along from image and exhibit to another. I didn't feel I was being urged to follow a path; the path chosen was the path." A fourth wrote: "The path I took to look at the piece was to examine all of the artwork [on the gallery walls] as a framing device, so that I could enjoy how it was used."

What did they make of it? One audience member thought it was like a horoscope in that the meaning made reflected the audience member who made it. Another wrote: "I was hyper-aware of my brain trying to make meaning and see patterns in everything. So the 'meaning' that I took was being conscious of my own instinct to see patterns—my instinct was to see patterns even in the roll of the dice." A third wrote: "For me, the piece was about the urge to find meaning/structure/narrative/content within the random patterns of our daily life and of the universe. Humans are hardwired to find meaning; it's part of what makes us the beings we are. It's why we love to hear stories. It's why even the least educated among us can spend hours a day staring at a television screen following narrative structures; we crave it. Your piece foregrounded that desire through its content (the actual discussions within the playlets, the thrusts of the musical and choreographic pieces) and its structure (the random stringing together of disparate units that invariably led to some sense of pace and flow, whether intended or not). Even pieces like 4:33 or the #TweetDances are, at base [sic], exercises in foregrounding the search for meaning within the seemingly random. And obviously that's the whole point of a Rorschach Test." Another audience member wrote: "I didn't take away a meaning as much as a feeling, a sensation of freshness, as though a breeze had blown through my inclination for thinking about learning. In fact, in reflection, the "show" seemed to be more about behavior than meaning, as though looking at people on the street or in customary places and being a fly on their cranial walls." One of the priests at Judson wrote: "At Judson, we spend a lot of time talking about the question of 'fate' and 'divine providence' versus the 'free will' to which we post-enlightened folks cling so desperately. Beyond the sheer delight I took in the fun of individual scenes and your actors' performances, I was struck by how 'the roll of a die' was both a random act and a fixed act. The scenes were written and so we were in a fixed universe, but we were set to experience that universe in a completely random way. Randomness within a wholly non-random world."

Of course, if "Why You Shouldn't Study the Brain" is one of the twenty scenes, audiences receive a warning about the mistakes our brain makes in the act of making meaning of two diagrams: "Instead of allowing ourselves to see what's really there—a collection of lines, an assortment of shapes, our brain fills in information based on past experiences so that we perceive familiar shapes. I challenge you to see the strange, interesting shape that's *actually* there—you can't. Even when you tell yourself to do it, you can't. [...] Maybe it's too important to us to make *sense* of things. Make them neat. But think of all the shapes we'll never see because of the few that we know."

In *Readymade Cabaret* audiences became "co-creators, rather than receptacles" of the play, as one participant noted. This was true not only in the process of making the piece (creating the Dada poem, tweeting dance prompts, and rolling the dice) but in the ultimate sense the piece made: if both the audience's attempts to make meaning and the meanings they come up with are the subject and substance of the play, then the audience is itself the message. More accurately, the ways they interact, the rasic moments created, and the experiences and conclusions they come to are the message of immersive and participatory theatre.

REFERENCES:

Audience A. 2014. Email to the author. June.

Audience B. 2014. Email to the author. June.

Bharata. 1996. *The Natyasastra*. Translated by Adya Rangacharya. Delhi: Munshiram Manoharlal Publishers Pvt. Ltd.

Deshpande, G.T. 1989. *Abhinavagupta*. Delhi: The Sahitya Akademi.

Deutch, Elliott. 1981. "Reflections on Some Aspects of the Theory of Rasa," 214–225 in *Sanskrit Drama in Performance*, Rachel Van M Baumer and James R Brandon, Honolulu: University of Hawaii Press.

Fischer-Lichte, Erika. 2008. *The Transformative Power of Performance*. London: Routledge.

Gregg, Melissa, and Gregory J. Seigworth, eds. 2010. *The Affect Theory Reader*. Duke University Press Books. Kindle edition.

Hall, Edith. 2015. "Aristotle's Theory of Katharsis in Its Historical and Social Contexts." Manuscript draft.

Hurley, Erin. 2010. *Theatre & Feeling*. London: Palgrave-Macmillan.

Lee, Kristine Haruna. 2015. "Making Meaning Out of Nothing." *Culturebot*. 8 May. http://www.culturebot.org/2015/05/23904/making-meaning-out-of-nothing/. Accessed 5 January, 2016.

McConnell, Collin. 2014. "A Serious Banquet." *New York Theatre Now*. 10 June. http://nytheaternow.com/2014/06/10/a-serious-banquet/. Accessed 5 January, 2016.

Ranciere, Jacques. 2011 [2009]. *The Emancipated Spectator*. London: Verso.

Schechner, Richard. "Rasaesthetics." In Performance Theory, second edition. London: Routledge. Pp 333–367.

Silbiger, Sam. 2014. Analysis of *Three Sisters* for Drama in Performance Course.

White, Gareth. 2013. Audience Participation in Theatre: Aesthetics of the Invitation. London: Palgrave-Macmillan.

Printed in the USA
CPSIA information can be obtained
at www.ICGtesting.com
LVHW062033101023
760672LV00073B/2170